In a world of entre   :s
ground-breaking, h   .ds with
the world' (*Sunday Times*) with displaced artists centre stage.

Founded by playwrights Joe Murphy and Joe Robertson, Good Chance established its first temporary Theatre of Hope, an 11-metre geodesic dome, in the heart of the 'Jungle' refugee and migrant camp in Calais in 2015, promoting freedom of expression, creativity and dignity for everyone. Good Chance now creates powerful and provoking work including *The Jungle* and *The Walk with Little Amal*, and radical acts of solidarity like *Fly With Me* and *From Here On*. Their work sparks new connections and conversations across divides, through surprise and spectacle. They connect communities through art and explore the big issues of our time, including migration and the climate crisis, to make real change possible. Central to all of this is the development of displaced artists, to become an integral part of the UK's creative ecosystem.

Good Chance has delivered 550 events globally, reached 1.1 million audience members and active participants, given paid employment to over 750 artists and bespoke 1-2-1 support and employment to 150 artists with lived experience of displacement. The company are recipients of awards including the Southbank Sky Arts Award for Theatre, an Obie, an Empty Space Peter Brook Award, the Michael Nyqvist Award and the Genesis Prize.

Charity no. 1166833. Find out more at www.goodchance.org.uk, and follow @GoodChanceTheatre (Instagram and Facebook) and @GoodChanceCal (X) on social media.

Royal Shakespeare Company

The Royal Shakespeare Company has its roots in the nineteenth century when a local brewer, Charles Flower, boldly established a theatre in Stratford-upon-Avon. The company as we know it today was formed by Sir Peter Hall in 1961 with the aim of producing new plays alongside those of Shakespeare and his contemporaries. Across our three permanent theatres in Stratford – the Royal Shakespeare Theatre, the Swan Theatre and The Other Place – and indeed around the globe, our mission is to bring people together to experience stories that deepen our understanding of ourselves, each other and the world around us, and to bring joy. We believe everybody's life is enriched by culture and creativity. We have collaborated with generations of the very best theatre makers and we continue to nurture the talent of the future. Our transformative Creative Learning and Engagement programmes reach over half a million young people and adults each year.

Registered charity no. 212481
rsc.org.uk
@thersc

Kyoto

Joe Murphy grew up in Leeds and Joe Robertson grew up in Hull. They began writing plays together at university in 2011. Their short plays include *Fairway Manor* (Burton Taylor Studio, Oxford Playhouse), *Ten Bits on Boondoggling* and *Paper Play* (Edinburgh Fringe) and *Maria Popova* (Manchester festivals). In 2015, they established Good Chance in the 'Jungle' refugee and migrant camp in Calais, a space of expression where theatre, art, dance and music could be made. They lived there for seven months until the eviction of the southern half of the camp. Their first full-length play, *The Jungle*, based on their experience in Calais, opened at the Young Vic in 2017, before transferring to the West End (2018), New York (2019/2023), San Francisco (2019) and Washington DC (2023). In 2021, Good Chance co-created *The Walk*, an 8,000km moving festival of welcome from Syria to Manchester with Little Amal, a three-metre tall puppet based on a character from *The Jungle*.

by the same authors

THE JUNGLE

JOE MURPHY
and
JOE ROBERTSON

Kyoto

faber

First published in 2024
by Faber and Faber Limited
The Bindery, 51 Hatton Garden
London, EC1N 8HN

Typeset by Brighton Gray
Printed and bound in the UK by CPI Group (Ltd), Croydon CR0 4YY

All rights reserved
© Joe Murphy and Joe Robertson, 2024

Joe Murphy and Joe Robertson are hereby identified as authors
of this work in accordance with Section 77 of the
Copyright, Designs and Patents Act 1988

All rights whatsoever in this work, amateur or professional,
are strictly reserved. Applications for permission for any use
whatsoever including performance rights must be made in
advance, prior to any such proposed use,
to Judy Daish, United Agents Limited, 12–26 Lexington Street,
London W1F 0LE (email: jdaish@unitedagents.co.uk)

No performance may be given unless a licence
has first been obtained

This book is sold subject to the condition that it shall not,
by way of trade or otherwise, be lent, resold, hired out
or otherwise circulated without the publisher's prior consent
in any form of binding or cover other than that in which
it is published and without a similar condition including
this condition being imposed on the subsequent purchaser

A CIP record for this book
is available from the British Library

ISBN 978–0–571–39249–0

Printed and bound in the UK on FSC® certified paper in line with our continuing
commitment to ethical business practices, sustainability and the environment.
For further information see faber.co.uk/environmental-policy

4 6 8 10 9 7 5 3

Authors' Note

The series of negotiations that lead to the Kyoto Protocol is one of the great stories of our time. We have loved living in this world, reading every word about it we can find, and speaking to dozens of people who were there.

We were given a piece of advice during an early conversation with a legendary environmental figure, which we have been reminded of during rehearsals: 'Obviously you can't write a play covering a whole decade of global environmental negotiations . . .'

Two years later, for better or worse, it appears we have.

In condensing many years into a few hours of stage time, we had to make decisions to conflate events, imagine conversations and simplify the often fiendish complexities of climate science. None of those decisions were made lightly, and always with an attempt to balance historical accuracy with the need to tell a dramatically coherent story. We have attempted to capture as much of the spirit and essence of those years as our writing ability allowed.

For those interested in the history that inspired the play, there is a wealth of brilliant books, such as *Heroes of Environmental Diplomacy* (Joanna Depledge), *The Carbon War* (Jeremy Leggett), *The Kyoto Protocol: International Climate Policy for the 21st Century* (Oberthür and Ott), *Survival Emissions* (Mark Mwandosya) and *Merchants of Doubt* (Erik M. Conway) to name just a few, as well as many excellent documentaries, radio programmes and online sources.

Making a play is a little like making a protocol – it takes a long time, a lot of (recycled) paper, and a large village of exceptional people. We would like to thank everyone who has worked on *Kyoto* since early 2022. To the many people we spoke to who generously entrusted us with their professional, personal and emotional experiences. To Joanna Depledge, for her patience and faith in gently guiding two laypeople. To our extraordinary researcher and dramaturg Gemma, our very own 'Hero of Kyoto', whose tenacity and care pushed the play in directions none of us expected – as one UN figure said, she would have been indispensable in thrashing out the agreement in Kyoto. To Naomi, Philip, Sophie, Ammar, Emily, Dina, Mel, Hannah, Amir, Sule, Mardin and everyone at Good Chance whose passion and positivity is our most reliable source of renewable energy. To everyone at the RSC who saw promise in the play before it even existed. To our peerless directors Justin and Stephen, who have always encouraged and believed in us – their emotional and dramatic insight makes them the greatest people to be in any room with. To Jane, Lizzie, Aida, Rob and Tom, whose careful stewardship has kept everyone afloat in the rehearsal room. To Sonia, whose patience as we tucked ourselves away to write for hours on end is never underestimated, we are grateful for your love.

And to the incredible cast and company of *Kyoto*, both in production and during workshops, who have shepherded the play through its many rounds of multilateral negotiations, endless rewrites and (occasionally, misplaced) commas . . . Thank you.

J.M. and J.R.
May 2024

Kyoto, a co-production between Good Chance and the RSC, was first performed at the Swan Theatre, Stratford-upon-Avon, on 18 June 2024. The cast was as follows:

Don Pearlman Stephen Kunken
Shirley Jenna Augen
Raúl Estrada-Oyuela Jorge Bosch
Fred Singer Vincent Franklin
Bert Bolin / Al Gore / Ben Santer Dale Rapley
Secretariat Olivia Barrowclough
Kiribati Andrea Gatchalian
Saudi Arabia Raad Rawi
China Kwong Loke
USA Nancy Crane
Germany Ingrid Oliver
Tanzania Jude Akuwudike
UK / John Houghton Ferdy Roberts
Japan Togo Igawa

All other parts played by members of the company

Directors Stephen Daldry & Justin Martin
Set Designer Miriam Buether
Costume Designer Natalie Pryce
Lighting Designer Aideen Malone
Sound Designer Christopher Reid
Video Designer Akhila Krishnan
Composer Paul Englishby
Associate Director Jane Moriarty
Dramaturg Gemma Stockwood

Casting Director Julia Horan CDG
US Casting Jim Carnahan CSA
Spanish Casting Camilla-Valentine Isola
Dialect Coach Zabarjad Salam (Budgie)
Associate Video Designer & Programmer Iain Syme
Assistant Set Designer Hannah Ursula Schmidt
Trainee Director Thomas Tegento
Production Manager Ben Arkell
Costume Supervisor Sian Harris
Company Stage Manager Robert Walker
Deputy Stage Manager Lizzie Cooper
Assistant Stage Manager Aida Bourdis

FOR ROYAL SHAKESPEARE COMPANY
Production Coordinator Tom Dickinson
General Manager Rebecca Treanor
Executive Producer Griselda Yorke

FOR GOOD CHANCE
Production Assistant Amir Ibrahimi
Producer Sophie Ignatieff
Executive Director Naomi Popli

For Tom

Characters

The Seven Sisters*
Representatives of the world's biggest oil companies

Don Pearlman
American lawyer and CEO of the Climate Council

Shirley Pearlman
Don's wife

Raúl Estrada-Oyuela
Argentinian Diplomat to China / Chairman of COP1–3

Fred Singer
Atmospheric physicist, Global Climate Coalition (GCC)

Bert Bolin
Scientist and first Chairman of the Intergovernmental Panel on Climate Change (IPCC)

Ben Santer
American climate scientist

Al Gore
Vice President of the United States

---

* 'The Seven Sisters' was the nickname for the cartel of leading oil companies in the twentieth century: Anglo-Iranian (now BP), Royal Dutch Shell (Shell), Standard Oil of California (Chevron), Gulf Oil (Chevron), Texaco (Chevron), Standard Oil of New Jersey (Esso, then Exxon, then ExxonMobil) and Standard Oil of New York (Mobil, then ExxonMobil).

NATIONAL DELEGATIONS

China

Germany

Japan

Kiribati

Saudi Arabia

Tanzania

UK

USA

OTHER CHARACTERS

The Secretariat
Member of the UN Secretariat

John Houghton
Scientist from the UK Met Office

Observer
NGO Observer

Scientists, Observers and others

As well as named individual characters we also use country names to represent the changing nature of national delegations during the course of the IPCC negotiations.

Setting

The action of the play takes place between 1989 and 1997.

KYOTO

I don't think writers are sacred, but words are. They deserve respect. If you get the right ones in the right order, you can nudge the world a little.

Tom Stoppard, *The Real Thing*

Note

/ indicates an interruption

Act One

ONE

Thunder and lightning. The Seven Sisters enter and encircle a wellbore.

Seven Sisters
    Down there, where the fuels do boil,
    Where thick black tar transforms to oil,
    There, there are rich spoils for all.

    Ancient fossils of all shapes and sizes;
    Pretty coals, slick oils, magical gases,
    Which, when well-bored, bear untold prizes.

    Of all this, we Seven Sisters speak,
    We Seven Sisters sing,
    Of the profit our natural resources bring.

    Down we drill for you this hour,
    Extracting one of such antique power
    That he'll frack right up your ivory tower.

    In the seams of history his name is curled,
    But we'll show you, when his story's told,
    How one man's emissions can choke up the world.

    One man we drilled and refined to burn them,
    One fossil, we know you've never heard of him,
    A lawyer, called Don Pearlman.

Another thunderclap. And they are gone.

TWO

Don Pearlman enters. He lights a Dunhill. Speaks in a familiar tone with the audience.

Don I think we can all agree on one thing: the times you live in are fucking awful. Everywhere you look there's some kind of disagreement, something angry, something vicious, something acutely horrible. There's some maladjusted kid, sticking a knife into his teacher. Or a bunch of refugees suffocated in the back of a truck. Or a thousand limbless civilians blown up inside a theatre. A politician leaking blood on the sidewalk, dying, shrieking, shot. There's food shortages, runaway inflation, culture wars, real wars, race riots, fake news, insane insurrections, global pandemics . . . And, on top of all that, a planet in literal fucking meltdown. And if you're a guy like me looking at a time like now, the main thing you think is, fuck man . . . the 1990s were freakin' *glorious*.

This was the End of History, as one smart-ass put it. The Cold War was over. The American way of life had prevailed. The World had a Trade Center that towered over Wall Street, and the only thing that kept us up at night was the Millennium fucking Bug. That's right, folks. The road ahead had the glint of gold. I see it, and I want to live there. But it's a fantasy. And it's silly to live in a fantasy. I suspect we can all agree on that. Even in this, your golden age of disagreement.

Now, the story you're about to see is true, but as a lawyer I have to say that some scenes and characters have been invented for dramatic purposes. And I know what people like you think of lawyers like me. You theatre, artsy, liberal types who pay your bills in empathy. But none of your concerns interest me. I'm the only one who can tell this story. Because I'm the only one who was there. Start to finish, I saw it all. Did it all. Fought for it all. And you may not like it all, but if you want to know it all, you can't have it all your own way.

The Capitol Building, Washington DC. 20 January 1989.
George H. W. Bush's inauguration speech.

George H. W. Bush There is a man here who has earned a lasting place in our hearts and in our history.

Don As the nineties dawn was about to break, I was saying farewell to the last great President America ever had.

George H. W. Bush President Reagan, on behalf of our Nation, I thank you for the wonderful things that you have done for America.

Applause.

Don I'd served under Ronald Reagan at the Department of Energy for seven beautiful years, and this morning I take my seat on the front porch of democracy for the last time, to witness a peaceful transfer of power. Remember those?

George H. W. Bush I come before you and assume the Presidency at a moment rich with promise. / We live in a peaceful, prosperous time. But we can make it better. For a new breeze is blowing. And a world refreshed by freedom seems reborn. For in man's heart, if not in fact, the day of the dictator is over . . .

Applause. The speech continues as the Seven Sisters enter.

First Sister 'A world refreshed by freedom seems reborn . . .' That is a classic. You must feel proud?

Don I played a small part. But we left the world a better place. And isn't that the point?

First Sister What's next?

Second Sister We hear you're joining Patton Boggs as a Partner?

Third Sister Now there's a law firm to shiver the bones.

Second Sister You must be drowning in potential clients.

Don I am. But first I've promised my wife a long vacation.

Fourth Sister Such a good husband, Don. Good family man. How is Shirley?

How does he know Shirley's name . . . ?

Don She's . . . fine, thank you. Excited to have me home.

Second Sister Potomac is beautiful this time of year.

Don It is.

First Sister Nice to spend time with the kids.

Don It will.

Fourth Sister And how are Stephanie and . . .

Don Brad.

Fourth Sister Brad. How are they?

Beat.

Don You all have a great day.

George H. W. Bush And so today a chapter begins, a small and stately story of unity, diversity, and generosity – shared, and written, together. Thank you. God bless you and God bless the United States of America.

Applause. Don goes to leave but a Sister steps in front of him.

First Sister How closely do you follow the United Nations, Don?

Don Fairly closely.

First Sister We follow it very closely.

Don We?

First Sister We represent a broad church of voices from the American business community. You may know that a few months ago, a couple of little UN groups got together and formed a bigger group. The IPCC. The Intergovernmental Panel / on –

Don – Climate Change.

First Sister Very closely. Now, these UN folk have gotten into their heads some interesting ideas, and they're doing a lot of talking right now, spending a lot of taxpayers' money, leading up to a big hoo-ha next November –

Fifth Sister *The World Climate Conference.*

First Sister Where we believe they may try to make some kind of Declaration. Some kind of commitment to targets and timetables.

Second Sister We really hate those words.

First Sister We feel that without proper oversight, words like 'targets' and 'timetables' will be used to harm us.

Second Sister To harm America, Don.

Sixth Sister Can we get you a drink?

Don Oh, no, I'm –

First Sister (*giving him a drink*) We wanna make sure our interests are represented in those conversations.

Don I can't imagine your interests aren't represented already.

First Sister We do fund a group. The Global Climate Coalition. But they're mostly shopfront guys. We want a man in the room.

Sixth Sister Someone under the hood, getting their hands dirty.

Second Sister Gotta keep that breeze blowing, Don.

Fifth Sister Freedom. Freedom to choose.

Don Why me?

First Sister We need a guy who can talk under water, you know?

Seventh Sister You're one of Washington's best lawyers. You're an excellent strategist.

Third Sister And you're across the subject. You were Don Hodel's Chief of Staff at Energy for seven years, for God's sake!

Don You know Don's answer to the hole in the ozone? Wear more sunscreen.

They all laugh.

Second Sister Gotta love that guy!

Third Sister He was your high school rival, wasn't he? The Two Dons –

Don How do you know that?

First Sister As you can see, we are taking this very seriously.

Pause.

Don I'm flattered. Really, I am. But I have a lot of offers to consider. And I made that promise to my wife.

First Sister Dip your toe in the water, Don. And if it's too hot, you take Shirley on that vacation you always promised. On us.

THREE

Inaugural Ball. Shirley enters holding a copy of TIME *magazine.*

Shirley My God, I just spent a half hour being jaw-jawed by the Editor-in-Chief of *TIME*. Who goes to an inaugural ball to push their darn magazine? And get a load of this. Instead of a Man of the Year, 1989 has a Planet of the Year.

'The Endangered Earth'! I said, trust *TIME* to pick a Planet of the Year before a Woman of the Year!

She laughs. Don doesn't respond.

You've got your coat on. The President hasn't even got here yet.

Don He already left. He was only here five minutes.

Shirley Oh, Don. Did you meet anyone else? Charlton Heston's still here . . .

Don Just some folk looking for help.

Shirley What kind of folk?

Don Oh . . . another special interest group.

Shirley What kind of help?

Don (*taking* TIME) Let me see that.

Beat.

Shirley (*as Don reads* TIME) You know, maybe we should split. Start our vacation early. I'll sure be happy to see the back of these things, won't you? Donald?

Don Uh-huh . . .

Shirley We always said, after Reagan's second inauguration, / you said . . .

Don I know, / I know –

Shirley We have enough money. We've made good investments. We can relax, for a moment.

Don Have you read this?
  (*Reading* TIME.) 'One generation passeth away, and another generation cometh: but the earth abideth forever.'

Shirley Ecclesiastes.

Don When the fuck did *TIME* open with a quote from the Tanakh? 'No, not forever . . . This year the earth spoke, like God warning Noah of the deluge.' Is this about the droughts?

Shirley I thought this year would be Mr Gorbachev.

Don 'Its message was loud and clear, and suddenly people began to listen, to ponder what portents the message held . . .' This is new.

Shirley Oh.

Don What?

Shirley You're interested. I can always tell. You look suddenly very serious.

FOUR

Don And I suppose *TIME* has piqued my interest because I'm reading it, devouring it actually, on a flight across the Atlantic ocean, Ecclesiastes echoing in my ears, to check into a country hotel in Berkshire, England, where I'm surrounded by –

Berkshire, England. May 1990. Scientists' Meeting.

Estrada One hundred leading scientists of the world.

Don turns to see a rotund, moustached man looking around for something, and also holding a copy of TIME. *This is Raúl Estrada. Estrada offers Don his hand.*

Raúl Estrada.

Don Are you a scientist?

Estrada God no! Argentinian Ambassador to China.

Don What's the Argentinian Ambassador to China doing at a climate conference in England?

Estrada Looking for a seat. I was the only diplomat available. Everyone else was mysteriously on vacation.

Don Go figure. So who's running this show?

Bert Bolin enters.

Estrada Bert Bolin. Grandfather of the modern climate movement. In '85 he held a summit in the Austrian Alps which led to the creation of the IPCC, which Bert now chairs. Sorry, I'm still playing catch up.

Don Join the club. There's a seat over there.

Estrada Ah! Thank you.

Estrada takes his seat as Bolin addresses the room.

Bolin The world needs to make its mind up. Governments will soon meet in Sweden to turn our Scientists' Report into the IPCC's First Assessment. We must decide now what that report will tell them. So what are we certain of?

Houghton We know that gases in the earth's atmosphere produce a natural greenhouse effect. We know that as the concentration of those gases increases, so does the earth's temperature.

Singer Perhaps . . .

Houghton Come now, we've known this since 1847. We know that man-made emissions are greatly accelerating this effect, and that immediate reductions in such emissions of sixty to eighty per cent are required to stabilise concentrations at 1990 levels.

Singer I'm sorry, but this is ridiculous. We have no goddam clue how carbon behaves in the atmosphere, much less what cuts are needed for stabilisation!

Houghton Have you read the science?

Singer This isn't science, it's guess work! Pin the tail on the big green donkey.

Houghton All the world's computer models say the same thing.

Singer I've seen your models. They couldn't even tell the goddam time. The climatic system has trillions of inputs but you feed a dozen into your little magic model until it tells you exactly what you want it to say.

Houghton That sounds like an accusation of scientific fraud. (*To Bolin.*) Even the tiniest changes could trigger catastrophic feedback loops we cannot yet predict. I want it in the report that we may be talking about the end of life on earth as we know it!

Singer I want it in the report that your models are a piece of shit.

Houghton (*packing his bag and leaving*) I've had enough of this. We should not be giving this 'scientist' a platform!

Bolin I can see there is a variety of strongly held opinions.

Don Not kidding.

Bolin Let's take five minutes.

The meeting adjourns. Estrada finds Don.

Estrada What have we let ourselves in for, eh?

Don Tell me about it.

Estrada Forgive me, I never asked who you were. Let me guess. American. You're not a scientist, so . . . Politician . . . ? Journalist . . . ? Chauffeur? Only joking.

Don Don Pearlman. Lawyer.

Estrada A lawyer! Me too.

Singer (*to Don*) Ah, the reinforcements! They told me you were coming. Fred Singer.

Don I don't think this is for me.

Estrada No?

Don Come on. The Berlin Wall just fell. Tiananmen Square. This is hysterical nerds arguing about computer models. No offence.

Singer Oh, none taken. We're supposed to be scientists but as you can see these discussions are more like dealing with the Church.

Estrada Does that make you Galileo?

Singer Dunno. Who's it make you?

Estrada A mere layperson.

Don Is there anything in what they're saying?

Singer Is the world about to end? Like everything in science, it's possible. It's possible that the speed of light in a vacuum isn't constant. It's possible quantum mechanics predicts a multiverse. It's possible that aliens land in my backyard every night and eat my roses. But until you show me concrete evidence, I'll still scatter my slug pellets and hope for the best. You can't rip up civilisation on a hypothesis.

Singer exits.

Estrada I don't know, Mr Pearlman. Something tells me these nerds are about to make the Berlin Wall look like a . . . 'cerca de estacas . . .' How do you say . . . ? Picket fence! Let's grab a drink some time. Maybe in Sweden?

Estrada exits.

FIVE

Don So I spend three months reading every book on climate I can get my hands on – which is fucking arduous, I can tell you – before landing in Sundsvall, Sweden where governments of the world meet to debate the Scientists' Report.

Sundsvall, Sweden. August 1990. IPCC Plenary Session.

Singer (*to Don*) 'The world needs to make its mind up' – you're gonna hear that a lot. But the world doesn't have a mind to make up. It's a mindless mess of two hundred very different nation states. The bloc system is the UN's attempt to resolve this problem.

Bolin (*gavelling the meeting to order*) You have all now read the Scientists' Report. Our job today is to turn it into the IPCC First Scientific Assessment. Who would like to begin?

(*Seeing a flag.*) The Distinguished Delegate of the Federal Republic of Germany.

Singer In the rich corner: the wets of the European Community. Moral divas of the international stage – communists and homosexuals mostly.

Germany (*German*) The Report is clear. Man-made climate change is real / and the threat it presents is great.

Don A little help here? I don't speak European.

Singer (*listening in his earphone*) Germany says it believes in climate change. No surprises there. Their delegations are crammed with enviros.

Don Enviros?

Singer Our nickname for the watermelons.

Don Watermelons?

Singer Our nickname for the enviros. Green on the outside –

Don Red in the middle?

Singer Got it in one.

Germany (*German*) We propose unbracketing the following line: 'Climate change will cause negative impacts.'

Singer They want to unbracket the line, 'Climate change will cause negative impacts'.

Don Unbracket?

Singer If a sentence is in brackets it's still up for debate. When the brackets are removed, it means everyone agrees.

This is all about language, Don. Punctuation. Down to the last comma. But I don't need to tell that to a lawyer.

Bolin The Distinguished Delegate of Japan.

Japan (*Japanese*) Japan does not feel / that the science is clear enough to make such a concrete statement, Mr Chairman. We should err on the side of caution until they are more certain in their findings.

Singer Then the more rational JUSSCANNZ –

Don Just what?

Singer The UN loves an acronym, Don. Japan, US, Switzerland, Canada, Australia, Norway, New Zealand. JUSSCANNZ. Or as I like to call them, 'Just Kick the Can Down the Road . . .' They want those brackets to stay exactly where they are.

Bolin (*seeing a flag*) The Distinguished Delegate of China.

Singer And in the poor corner, the developing world . . .

China (*Mandarin*) The Report is clear about the negative impacts of global warming, but what about the benefits?

Consternation in the room.

Singer Naughty! China's asking about the *benefits* of global warming!

China (*Mandarin*) We propose changing the line to / 'Climate Change will cause negative *and* positive impacts.'

Singer They want the line to read 'Climate change will cause both negative *and* positive impacts.' A customary grenade from Dr No.

Don Dr No?

Singer Dr Shukong Zhong. Speaks better English than the Brits, says 'no' better than the Yanks. China's part of the biggest bloc, the G77 plus China. One hundred and twenty-eight developing countries of the world, unite!

Bolin The Distinguished Delegate of Tanzania.

Singer Or not . . .

Tanzania I have studied the Scientists' Report in great detail –

Don Makes two of us.

Tanzania – and with the greatest respect to our G77 partners, found no reference to positive impacts. Surely we should listen to the experts?

Singer In theory, countries in a bloc share circumstances, attitudes. But that many in one bloc? And one insists on top billing? That's when 'making your mind up' gets complex.

Bolin The Distinguished Delegate of the USA.

USA Never thought I'd say this, Mr Chairman, but our Chinese friends may have a point. Did the scientists even consider possible benefits?

Bolin Tanzania has the floor.

Tanzania It's possible a warmer world will benefit some kinds of agriculture, but for the most part it will bring devastation, especially for the developing world. Increased temperatures, extreme weather, ecosystem damage, sea-level rise. We have to see the bigger picture here!

USA Oh, I see the bigger picture, alright. I can't be the only one looking forward to a longer summer vacation by the pool . . . !

This joke gets a mixed reception. The meeting starts to fall apart.

Bolin Alright. Let's take a short break.

He gavels. Kiribati catches up with USA.

Kiribati (*Gilbertese*) Excuse me, madam? Can I speak with you for a moment? I'm from Kiribati.

USA English, please?

Kiribati I'm from Kiribati.

USA Where?

Singer (*to Don*) Some light entertainment?

Kiribati Kiribati. A coral atoll in the Pacific Ocean. If this report is true, my home will be underwater soon. I want an apology. This is no summer vacation by the pool.

USA It's just a joke.

Kiribati No, it's life or death. The report says that without an eighty per cent reduction in emissions, sea levels could rise / by six centimetres a decade –

Don An eighty per cent reduction?! Do you have any idea what that would mean for world civilisation? We'd all be back in the eighteenth century. Where did you say you were from?

Kiribati Kiribati.

Don Right. And how many people live there?

Kiribati Eighty thousand.

Don Are you honestly proposing we completely destroy the global economy, wreck the lives of six billion people, for one small island of eighty thousand?

Kiribati It isn't just one island! There are many other / island states facing the same –

Bolin gavels the meeting back to order.

Bolin The Distinguished Delegate of the United States.

USA How about a compromise: 'Climate change will cause both positive and negative impacts, but the negative ones will dominate'?

Germany (*German*) Mr Chairman! This is ridiculous! We propose the sentence stays unaltered!

Saudi Arabia Europe once again preaching from her pulpit.

Bolin The Distinguished Delegate of Saudi Arabia.

Saudi Arabia Curious she never complained about fossil fuels when the tap was running freely her way. Now we've fitted a meter, she wants to ban them altogether! Is it really climate change she's concerned about, or other countries profiting from their own natural resources and finally catching them up?

Arguments break out.

Don Who's he?

Singer OPEC. The Organisation of Petroleum Exporting Countries.

Taking Don to meet Saudi Arabia.

Mr Pearlman, meet Mohammed Al Sabban. Head of the Saudi Arabian delegation. And the reason you're in Sweden.

Saudi Arabia Your friends speak very highly of you, Mr Pearlman. What makes you think you can help us?

Don I'm not sure I can.

Saudi Arabia Oh?

Don Why would you need a Washington attorney? There are enough lawyers here already.

Singer The US created the UN in its image, don't forget that. We had the idea, we pay for it and it's HQ'd on the banks of the East River, Midtown Manhattan.

Saudi Arabia Don't worry, Fred. This we never forget.

Singer I'd have thought a Washington attorney is exactly what you need.

Saudi Arabia (*to Don; a challenge*) What do you suggest?

Don I got nothing. I mean, if no one can agree, just cut the goddam line.

Bolin (*gavelling the meeting to order*) It's four o'clock in the morning! If there are no more serious proposals, let us please unbracket the sentence and –

Saudi Arabia Saudi Arabia has a proposal.

Bolin The Distinguished Delegate of Saudi Arabia.

Saudi Arabia If agreement cannot be reached on the sentence, it should be omitted.

Shocked, the room looks to Saudi Arabia.

USA We second this.

China So do we.

Japan And us.

Bolin Seriously? Very well. The sentence, 'Climate change will cause negative impacts' is omitted from the report, which I hereby recommend for consideration in Geneva.

Bolin gavels. A shocked meeting adjourns.

Singer A Washington attorney has his uses after all.

Saudi Arabia (*exiting*) See you in Geneva. On us.

Singer You could get the hang of this, don't you think?

SIX

Geneva. November 1990. The World Climate Conference.

Don Geneva. The World Climate Conference, where Ministers will turn the First Scientific Assessment into a Declaration to act. I'm sorta getting used to these UN fun fairs. The circus really comes to town. Delegates from hundreds of countries descend like locusts, sucking up every hotel room in a thirty-mile radius. Flights full. Traffic at a standstill. Saving the earth is a filthy business.

A small meeting of Ministers and Don, who sits behind Saudi Arabia, advising him.

Bolin When you requested a 'small side-meeting', I didn't realise we could have held it in a broom cupboard.

USA Those big groups can be so ineffective. We might finally make some progress here.

Germany We propose unbracketing this sentence: 'Countries are urged to take immediate actions to control the risks of climate change.' Surely we can all agree on this?

Saudi Arabia No, no, no, too strong.

USA What does it even mean? 'Countries are *urged* . . .'

Germany I'm sorry, but this *is* urgent. I feel urged.

USA I don't feel urged. Do you feel urged?

Saudi Arabia No, I don't feel urged at all.

Don (*to Saudi Arabia*) Cut 'urged'.

Saudi Arabia Cut 'urged'.

USA Seconded.

Germany 'Urged' is a red line for us.

Don Encouraged?

USA Invited?

Saudi Arabia Coerced?

Germany No, we should all feel 'urged'!

Don (*to Saudi Arabia*) Okay, then we have to cut 'immediate'.

Saudi Arabia Cut 'immediate'.

Bolin 'Countries are urged to take actions to control the risks of climate change.'

USA What are these 'actions'? An idealistic promise made today could close a factory in Detroit tomorrow.

Don (*passing a note to Saudi Arabia*) And add –

Saudi Arabia 'With emphasis on actions that would be economically beneficial as well.'

Bolin 'Countries are urged to take actions to control the risks of climate change with emphasis on actions that would be economically beneficial as well.'

USA No Regrets. We second that.

Germany Rather takes the bite out of it, wouldn't you say?

USA It's realistic.

Germany Can we at least say 'with *initial* emphasis'?

Bolin Really? 'Countries are urged to take actions to control the risks of climate change with *initial* emphasis on actions that would be economically beneficial –'

Don And socially beneficial.

Bolin looks up at Don.

Bolin 'And socially beneficial as well.'

USA Fine.

Germany Fine.

Saudi Arabia looks to Don, who shrugs.

Saudi Arabia Fine.

Bolin Rejoice! The line – or whatever is left of it – is unbracketed. If there's nothing else –

Don I got something else. This line, 'Sea-level rise *would* threaten survival.' Should be *could*.

Saudi Arabia Agreed.

USA Agreed.

Bolin I must point out that only delegates and certified NGO observers can propose amendments.

Saudi Arabia He's with me. He's with me!

Bolin Very well. 'Sea-level rise *could* threaten survival.' Let's see what Conference has to say.

The Conference Hall. Bolin gavels the meeting to order.

The Distinguished Delegate of Kiribati.

Kiribati The text is completely different to yesterday.

Don And then the ambush.

Kiribati Why?

Bolin A smaller working group continued negotiations into the night.

Kiribati Why was Kiribati not invited?

Bolin A member of your bloc was present.

Kiribati Saudi Arabia?

Confers with its partners.

Kiribati would like to make an announcement.

Bolin The floor is yours.

Kiribati We, along with a large group of similar nations, have formed a new bloc. The Alliance of Small Island States will henceforth negotiate together.

Shock around the room. Don is on high alert.

USA We object, Mr Chairman! You can't just make a new bloc!

Kiribati Why not?

USA The bloc system has worked perfectly well for forty years –

Kiribati The Small Islands disagree. We feel marginalised and ignored. When you speak to Kiribati, you're no longer speaking to one small island of eighty thousand, but to an intergovernmental organisation of thirty-nine low-lying nation states stretching from the Caribbean to the Pacific. And AOSIS is open to anyone who would like to join.

Saudi Arabia They already have an acronym?

USA Mr Chairman –

Bolin I am not aware of any UN convention that forbids countries from working together. I daresay that's sort of the point.

Kiribati Thank you, Mr Chairman. It seems the Declaration has had its teeth removed. This sentence, for example: 'Sea-level rise *could* threaten survival.' Not for us, Mr Chairman. For us, it is death. We propose replacing '*could*' with '*would*'.

USA The Declaration has undergone many long hours of negotiation. We oppose any further changes at this stage.

Saudi Arabia Seconded.

Kiribati Oh, we're just getting started. Where have all the references to CO_2 gone?

Don rushes a note to Saudi Arabia.

Saudi Arabia (*reading*) If we rebracket a sentence that has been agreed, then we rebracket the whole Declaration!

Kiribati And all references to targets and timetables have vanished. Perhaps the Secretariat is having problems with its photocopier?

USA Can we just agree the goddam Declaration? Some of us have planes to catch. We'll be here for days if we continue discussing matters of little substance!

A stunned pause.

Don Something changes in the room.

Kiribati Permit me to say the unsayable, Mr Chairman. There is one country among us with less than five per cent of the world's population, responsible for over a third of its greenhouse gas emissions. It prides itself on world leadership, but has shown none at these talks. I'm only sorry that its Distinguished Delegate does not consider our survival a matter of substance.

Don Then it begins.

Kiribati On second thoughts, Mr Chairman, the conditional tense is no longer sufficient for us. Sea-level rise *will* threaten our survival.

Don Western Samoa rises first. They support Kiribati.

Kiribati It *will* drown our crops.

Don Then the Republic of Nauru. They second this and want it in the minutes –

Kiribati It *will* salinate our fresh water supplies.

Don Followed by Trinidad and Tobago, Barbados, Bangladesh, the Bahamas –

Kiribati It *will* bleach our coral reefs and kill our mangrove forests.

Don Tanzania –

Tanzania – supports the Island States. The developing world will not be brushed aside!

Kiribati It *will* erode our coastlines and destroy our homes –

Don Mauritius, St Lucia.

Kiribati It *will* displace us from our land.

Don The Cook Islands, the Maldives.

Kiribati It *is* displacing us.

Don The Federated States of Micronesia.

Kiribati And we *will not* drown in silence.

Don A tidal wave of resentments, old and new, floods the Conference Hall. Kiribati has burst a dam.

USA We refuse to debate the foundations of American freedom!

China Perhaps American freedom is ill-suited to the challenges of the future!

Don *What?*
   (*Rushing a note to Saudi Arabia.*) I try to close the floodgates.

Saudi Arabia We demand that proceedings be cut off –

Don But it's too late.

Arguments break out between the developed and developing worlds. A single flag rises. Bolin gavels until there is silence.

Bolin The Distinguished Delegate of Argentina?

Estrada Forgive my English, Mr Chairman, but might I suggest to delegates that we keep our *eyeses on the prizes*?

Confused laughter pierces the tension. Estrada chuckles.

What did I tell you?! It seems to me we may be closer than we think. If the USA agrees to replace 'could' with 'would' . . .

The USA confers, then nods.

. . . will the Island States agree to the Declaration?

Kiribati confers, then finally:

Kiribati For the sake of compromise . . . The Alliance of Small Island States agrees.

Everyone looks to Estrada. How did he do that?

Bolin Then it is decided. The next time we meet, we will be negotiating a Convention.

He gavels, and the meeting adjourns.

SEVEN

Don and Shirley at home.

Don I just couldn't figure out why I was so drawn to it. Until that moment. In that moment I saw the world change. Countries you've never even heard of rising up and facing us down. 'American Freedom is ill-suited to the challenges of the future.' They hate us.

Shirley Who are 'they'?

Don Exactly. Fucking Kiribati . . . Is this what we fought the Cold War for? For an American citizen to be ordered by unelected foreign governments in some shitty room in Geneva that he can't buy the things he wants to buy, drive the car he wants to drive, start the business he wants to run. We don't let our own government dictate that to us. There'd be riots on the goddam streets. What they're deciding in those rooms is a direct challenge to the idea of America. To American freedom. Well, sometimes freedom means war.

Shirley Don't use that word. People die in wars.

Don No one's gonna die. But other things will, if someone doesn't stand up.

Shirley And you think that's you?

Don Why shouldn't it be me?

Shirley Because once you start, you don't know how to stop. At least in DC they kick you out after two terms. You have other choices. Closer to home. Closer to Stephanie. Closer to Brad.

Don You don't choose public service, Shirl. It chooses you. This is about our way of life. It's about Brad and Stephanie.

Shirley It'll be a lot. That's all I'm saying. You missed your last check-up.

Don No, I didn't.

Shirley I do the insurance, Donald.

Don I'm fifty-two, Shirl. I'm fine.

Shirley Fine. You're fine. But this isn't public service. This isn't the Department of Energy. These people will use you for all you're worth, and when you're spent and wheezing on the sidewalk, who'll be there?

Don looks at her directly. Shirley shakes her head.

I wanted us to travel the world. Not the climate conference circuit.

Don Geneva, Shanghai . . . Bonn –

Shirley Bonn!

Don They're beautiful cities.

Shirley All that concrete.

Don Sure, it'll be hard. Long flights every week. Constant talking. Constant drinks, dinners, *events*. But if I take my camera, it might even feel like a vacation.

Shirley Don't lobby me, Don. It might work with Kiribati, but not with your wife.

Don So what do you think?

The Seven Sisters enter.

First Sister We're thrilled, Don. Just thrilled.

Second Sister Two years of UN claptrap for a Declaration that declares nothing.

Third Sister No targets, no timetables.

Don No. There's something happening. Countries are uniting. Different countries. Countries that don't like each other. Countries that don't know each other. Countries that are currently at war with each other are agreeing. About the fucking weather. If I'm going to do this –

First Sister You're gonna do this?

Don *If* I am, I'm going to need a lot of support. Unlimited.

First Sister Sure thing.

Don Anonymity for my wife and kids.

First Sister Consider it done.

Don And something else. I need a ticket to the conference floor. I need an NGO.

Fourth Sister Fossil Fuels Forever?

Don Something neutral. Something that doesn't give away our position. Something like . . . The Climate Council.

EIGHT

First Sister Ladies and gentlemen, please welcome the CEO of the Climate Council, Donald H. Pearlman.

Champagne corks pop! The launch party for Don's new NGO, with the Sisters, Shirley, Singer, Saudi Arabia, and others.

Don It seems only yesterday we were all quite content, sitting on democracy's porch, with that gentle breeze blowing over us. But the breeze has turned into a blizzard, folks, and the front step's hurting our ass. Every day now scientists try to tell us how to live our lives. Every day they tell us that the oil that powers our lives is a threat to life itself. Well, let me tell you an uncomfortable truth, people. This . . .

Holds up a glass of water.

. . . is oil.

Points at a wall.

This is oil.

At someone's chair.

This is oil.

Don goes round the whole room, pointing at objects, each the product of oil-powered manufacturing. Every object he points at, he chants: 'This is oil!' The audience joins in.

Even this. All of this! Is oil. It is the water, the wine, the blood. It is the American sacrament.

Sisters Amen!

Don The Climate Council exists to do one thing. Prevent targets and timetables for the reduction of greenhouse gas emissions. There are five two-week sets of talks between now and the Rio Earth Summit next June. That's just ten weeks, ladies and gentlemen. You ready? Are you ready?!

Cheers.

Round One. Chantilly, Virginia. A sweaty February heatwave, the hottest since records began.

Chantilly, Virginia. February 1991. First round of talks.

Bolin (*gavelling meeting to order*) We have all agreed we must act. Now we must decide how.
(*Seeing a flag.*) The Distinguished Delegate of the United States.

Don Strategy One. Be present in every second of the negotiations.

USA I want to say this to the developing world: we heard you in Geneva. And we hope our Action Plan addresses your concerns.

Don When you're there every second of every day, meet everyone you see, write down every word you hear . . .

Bolin The Distinguished Delegate of Kiribati.

Don You get a sixth sense for where to sink the drill.

Hands a note to Saudi Arabia.

Wait for it . . .

Kiribati The Island States feel that this Action Plan is a good first step.

Don Wait for it . . .

Kiribati We propose meeting in a smaller working group to discuss it further.

Don Now!

Saudi Arabia We have some procedural questions about the working groups.

Don I love procedural questions. How many will there be? Who will chair them? What will they focus on?

Bolin One could focus on science. One on implementation. One on targets and timetables.

USA We don't feel the science is clear enough for targets and timetables.

China But that's the whole point of the convention?

USA If you're so concerned, where's China's target and timetable?

China We have four times more people, madam, and half of your emissions.

USA And how many coal-fired power plants did you build last week?

China We did not cause this problem. You did. China will not remain poor so that the world can breathe.

USA And the US won't make itself poor on the basis of a few scare stories.

Arguments break out.

Don Disagreement. It's like striking oil. An hour becomes a day. A day becomes a week. And before you know it, the heatwave has passed, the talks are over, and the only thing agreed is –

Bolin Two. There will be two working groups.

Don Conference adjourned.

Bolin gavels.

Round Two. Geneva.

Geneva. June 1991. Second round of talks.

Strategy Two. Challenge the science.

Singer enters with newspapers.

Singer Latest scientific findings.

Bolin, China, Kiribati and USA enter. Don and Singer hand them newspapers as they pass.

Double-page spread in the *New York Times*!

Don A little bedtime reading?

Bolin (*opening the meeting*) Thank you for taking part in this working group on America's Action Plan. I hope we can make considerable progress together.

USA and China are distracted by the newspaper.

Singer (*reading*) The latest models show that ocean evaporation and subsequent deposition on the ice caps will far outweigh glacial melting and thermal expansion.

Don (*reading*) 'Will global warming in fact slow down sea-level rise rather than speed it up?'

Singer Question mark.

Don I love a question mark.

USA I have to pass this by our scientists.

China Likewise.

USA and China exit.

Bolin No, wait . . . !

Don By the time they do, the damage is done. We've killed two weeks.

Bolin (*to Kiribati*) It always finds a way in.

Kiribati What does?

Bolin Oil.

Don Conference adjourned. Round Three. Nairobi.

Nairobi. September 1991. Third round of talks.
Secretariat enters with a pack of documents.

What is this?

Secretariat Japan's proposal to bridge the divide between the USA and China.

Japan We call it 'Pledge and Review'. Each nation makes an emissions Pledge that they, and they alone, decide. After five years, countries work together to help review each other's progress.

Don Is a Pledge legally binding?

Japan No, no. It's more a broad aim.

Don So what stops a country from breaking its pledge?

Japan A sense of mutual trust and shared responsibility . . .

Don Fascinating . . .

USA enters.

Strategy Three. Double diplomacy. Say one thing to one country, and something completely –
  (*Seeing USA.*) So Japan's proposal, Pledge and Review . . .

USA It looks good to us.

Don You know the whole thing was Made in China?

USA Don't be ridiculous.

Don (*looking over shoulder*) It's true. I heard Zhong pitch it privately weeks ago. It sounds voluntary, but there is no way in hell they're going to let you get away with breaking your pledge.

USA Fuckers!

USA exits. China enters.

Don And something completely different to –
(*Seeing China.*) Hey, Zhong. Pledge and Review?

China It could be a way forward for us.

Don I just thought you should know. It was Born in the USA.

China What?

Don Your growth is nine-point-two per cent, double the US, and that scares the shit out of them. Pledge and Review will allow them to keep doing whatever the hell they want.

China Fuckers!

The Conference Hall. Bolin gavels.

Bolin The Distinguished Delegate of China.

China We oppose Pledge and Review. The developing world doesn't need hollow promises. It needs targets and timetables from those who caused the problem.

USA The US opposes Pledge and Review too, albeit for completely different reasons. And as he knows full well, we will not negotiate targets and timetables. We're walking.

USA stands and exits.

Bolin No, no, wait! Let us discuss . . . !

Don But it's done. Conference adjourned. Round Four. Back to Geneva.

Geneva. December 1991. Fourth round of talks. The Conference Hall.

Bolin Our need for progress is becoming acute. I hope the Distinguished Delegate of Germany has a bright idea?

Germany A Carbon Tax. Instead of targets and timetables, developed countries simply pay a levy on the carbon we use. The more we use, the more we pay. Let the market decide. We know how much our American friends believe in the market –

USA We do.

Germany A Carbon Tax empowers individuals and businesses, and could help fund green projects in the developing world.

Bolin The Distinguished Delegate of Tanzania.

Tanzania We find this proposal very interesting.

USA As do we.

China And us.

Bolin This might be the breakthrough we've been looking for.

Don Strategy Four. Emphasise the costs of action.

Bolin The Distinguished Delegate of Saudi Arabia.

Saudi Arabia We have produced a document that costs the introduction of such a carbon tax.

Bolin Documents need to be submitted in advance / for the agenda –

Saudi Arabia It would mean economic devastation for oil-producing states –

Don And most of the developed world. While China burns all the fossil fuels it likes, the slim profit margins of rival American companies will disappear in a heartbeat. Factories will close, people will lose their jobs, single industry towns will collapse into poverty, families broken apart, education stymied, and America handicapped on the global stage.

USA (*continuing*) This is not a plan to prevent climate change. It's a plan to destroy America. We're walking!

USA leaves. Depressed groans from around the room.

Don Conference adjourned. Round Five. New York. The final round of talks.

New York. February 1992. Fifth round of talks. Don and Shirley's hotel room.

How do I look?

Shirley Younger, somehow. Like the old days.

Don You know, I think I might be really good at this.

Shirley The first time we met you told me you knew you wanted to work in politics from the age of five. Of course you're good at it.

Don I was thinking . . . Bobby Short . . .

Moves towards her, flirtatiously.

Late Night at the Cafe Carlyle?

Shirley Oh, shush! We'll never get tickets!

Don (*handing her two tickets*) We have a table booked at eight.

Shirley What have you done with my husband?

He kisses her and exits, leaving Shirley stunned.

Don Strategy Five. Influence domestic politics.

The United Nations. Don lights a cigarette and sits opposite USA.

You said in a working group yesterday that 'it's inevitable America will have to take the lead on targets and timetables'.

USA That was a private meeting.

Don Was that a wise concession to make?

USA I was among friends –

Don Friends? I don't see any friends around here. This is open warfare. We're in the trenches. It's black as pitch. And you're the idiot private who lights a cigarette and gives away our position. The President will hear about this.

USA Don't threaten me, Don –

Don Actually, he already has. My job here is to hold you accountable to the American people. Every word you say in every meeting. And I don't just send them to the President. I send them to every congressman, mayor and fucking postal clerk from Washington State to DC. Do you know what happens to that private? She gets shot in the head. Hey, Private!

Don fires an imaginary gun at USA.
The Conference Hall.

Bolin The Distinguished Delegate of the United States.

All eyes are on USA, who looks to Don, who nods.

USA We support action, just like everyone else.

Don But . . .

USA But it has to be No Regrets action that doesn't damage our way of life.

Don And . . .

USA And it must be shared across all nations. We cannot sign the Convention in its current form.

A furious reaction.

Don Perfect.

Jazz begins playing. Don puts on a bow tie. Shirley enters in a dress, and the two of them dance, while Don addresses us.

Conference adjourned. The talks end in failure. I arrive at the Rio Earth Summit where Ministers of the world meet to sign a Convention that barely exists.

Singer It's not just diluted. It's homeopathic.

Don No targets.

Singer No timetables.

Don (*to cheers*) And that, ladies and gentlemen, is what the Climate Council is all about.

Singer lights two cigarettes and hands one to Don.

Singer Good work, Don.

Don You worked for Philip Morris. Don't you ever worry? The C word?

Singer Most of the research on smoking is the definition of junk science. Besides, we'll have a cure before they know it.

Don You so sure?

Singer This is America, Don. How long did the Apollo programme take us, from launch to lunar landing? Eight years. The Transcontinental Railroad? Six years. The Manhattan Project? Three years. The Panama Canal. The automobile. The transistor. The satellite – that one was me personally! Vaccines. Antibiotics. The Human Genome Project. Silicon Valley. We'll figure it out. We always do.

NINE

Rio de Janeiro. June 1992. The Rio Earth Summit.

Don Rio de Janeiro. The city's teeming with delegates picking up favours, ideas, arrangements. This isn't Conference, it's Carnival. Politicians and priests, oil miners and ministers, fiscalists and physicists, all sweating the same human juice. Dancing in conversation. Chanting *convention, convention, convention* . . .

Shirley looks out over the city.

Shirley I've never seen anything more beautiful.

Don Neither have I.

Don takes a photo of Shirley, surprising her.

Shirley Oh, stop it. You know, you haven't looked so relaxed since . . . I don't even know when.

Don Things are going so well, maybe it is time for a little vacation.

Estrada Mr Pearlman!

Don Spoke too soon.

Shirley Grip and grin, Don. Grip and grin.

Don Raúl! This is my wife, Shirley.

Estrada Raúl Estrada.

Shirley It's lovely to meet you, Mr Estrada. I've heard so much about you.

Estrada I'm glad I made an impression. Are you excited for the Earth Summit?

Shirley Oh, I've really been looking forward to this one. I've never been to Rio.

Estrada You're going to love it. And for the biggest environmental summit in history. No more little meetings in smoky back rooms, eh, Don?

Hands Shirley an envelope as he exits.

The world is waking up!

Don He's right.

Shirley Well, he's lovely. And he's invited us to an *event*!

Don (*to us*) You never want to hear that word. And concern rises in me when the driver pulls out of our hotel and heads not to the city, but to the darkness, to the green, green darkness. The sun falls in front of the Redeemer. And at sixty miles per hour, by winding, narrowing roads, heading into thick forest, I realise I'm clutching on to my wife.

Shirley You're hurting my arm.

Don The driver senses my fear; he accelerates at speed.

Shirley Look at the size of those trees . . .

Don But all I'm thinking is how many degrees we're rising as we climb up to the canopy of the rainforest.

A clearing in the rainforest, full of people, some in costume.

And we emerge. A great clearing.

Stage Manager This is your Act One beginners' call!

Don Not just delegates, but artists too. There are artists everywhere. And this is the first moment on this climate roadshow that I feel real danger. That I sense true agreement may be staring at me from behind the trunks of these great trees.
(*To Shirley.*) This is becoming . . . fashionable.

Shirley (*handing him a handkerchief*) You're sweating.

Don A man steps into the clearing. Different from the rest. The audience parts.

Shirley Oh my God, it's Werner Herzog!

Don Who?

Shirley *Heart of Glass? Nosferatu the Vampyre?*

Don What are you saying?

Shirley He's a famous film director!

Don Oh, shit . . .

Shirley *A Midsummer Night's Dream*. Directed by Werner Herzog. In a rainforest!

Werner Herzog (*to the crowd*) Follow me.

Herzog leads the crowd into the rainforest.

Actor Ill met by moonlight, proud Titania . . .

Shirley Oh my God, it's promenade!

Don Promenade?

Shirley It means it moves!

Werner Herzog Sit.

Shirley and the crowd sit for the first scene. Don is finishing his cigarette.

Shirley Quick, it's about to start!

Don There's only one thing worse than a gruelling twelve-hour IPCC plenary session.

Shirley Donald?

Don And that's sitting down, on the fucking ground . . .

Shirley Don!

Don To watch a Shakespeare play.

Jungle noises. Green light washes over the stage. Actors enter.

Actor The seasons alter: the spring, the summer,
The childing autumn, angry winter, change
Their wonted liveries; and the mazed world,
By their increase, now knows not which is which . . .
(*Addressing Don.*) This same progeny of evils comes
From your debate, from your dissension.
You are their parent and original.

Don (*to Shirley*) I'm going for a piss.

TEN

Don finds a bar.

Don Double whisky, please.

Estrada Make that two.

Don Exit pursued by moustache.

Estrada Not enjoying the play?

Don Your Convention's on life support and you want a theatre review?

Don lights a cigarette. Offers one to Estrada, who accepts.

Honestly, I think it's a pretentious piece of shit.

Estrada Maybe our tastes aren't so different then! I love everything about Germany, except for its art.

Don Actors are just failed lawyers.

Estrada You have a sense of humour, Mr Pearlman.

Don Endangered species at the UN.

Estrada What did the Argentinian climate sceptic say to the climate scientist?

Pause.

Argentina isn't warming, it's bordering on Chile!

Don Almost as funny as when you pretend to forget English.

Estrada When what . . . ?

Don When you pretend to forget . . . Touché.

Estrada Humour is an underrated tool in brokering agreement.

Don Is that what you are, Raúl? A man who brokers agreement?

Estrada When I was fourteen years old, under the military junta, I was quite the dissident. Anti-government riots were my speciality. Every time the police would arrest me and every time my father would drive down to the station and pay my bail. I used to get so angry at him, talking and laughing with the officer who an hour earlier held my hands in chains. But then I realised what he was doing. He was creating in that police station a tiny zone of agreement. He taught me that it might be better to work for change from within, than always to be throwing stones from the outside. So I became a lawyer. Maybe we are not so different after all?

Don I work for Patton Boggs and Blow.

Estrada I've heard of it.

Don What have you heard?

Estrada hesitates.

Come on. What have you heard?

Estrada 'The biggest compliment you can pay a Patton Boggs partner is that he'll do anything for money.'

Beat.

Don So we're doing stories? I'm a Lithuanian Jew. My parents found freedom in America. When the world was killing us, America kept us safe. They sold furniture. We struggled. But I studied hard and got into Stanford. When Stanford apologetically explained they'd exceeded their 'Jew quota', I went two better and got into Harvard and Yale. That scar tissue, that's America, Raúl. The son of an immigrant shopkeeper can climb the Hill and walk into the White House. The biggest mistake you make is thinking this is about money. It isn't. You're not the only ones fighting for something.

Estrada Can we play a game?

Don A game?

Estrada draws an imaginary circle on the ground between them.

Estrada Humour me. Imagine this circle is our own tiny zone of agreement. The aim of the game is for me to get us both inside the circle. To do this, I will ask you questions. If the answer is yes, we take a step towards one another. If the answer is no, we take a step apart. Clear?

Don And if I neither agree nor disagree?

Estrada Such a lawyer, Don. You can stay where you are. Ready?

Don Sure.

Estrada First question. Do you agree that climate change is real?

Don thinks for a moment. Then takes a step towards Estrada.

Unexpected.

He steps towards Don.

Do you agree that human beings are to blame?

Don takes a step back.

Don I believe that climate change is a natural process of the earth warming and cooling over time.

Estrada steps back.

Estrada Alright. Do you agree we all have a responsibility for the world we live in?

Don takes a step towards him. Estrada too.

Do you also agree that some of us bear more responsibility than others?

Don doesn't move.

That's okay. But can you agree, and this is important, that some countries possess a greater capacity to meet those responsibilities than others?

Don takes a step towards him. Estrada too. They are one step away from the circle.

Final question. If it ever becomes clear that we do need to act, do you agree that we should, for the sake of your children and mine? And would you work with me to make sure that we do?

Don That's a lot of questions Raúl.

Don walks into the circle.

Estrada Then that is the Convention. 'Common but differentiated responsibilities'. A simple promise that if and when the time comes, those who can act, will. And I believe we will. I sense it in the . . . atmósfera?

Don Come on, Raúl.

Estrada The atmosphere. Touché.

Don You won't get anything past me. Like you running for Chairman.

Estrada I didn't think I needed to tell you that, Don. Of course you already know.

Shirley re-enters.

Shirley That was incredible. Turns out I *love* German art. Werner says we have to visit the theatre in Berlin.

Estrada That's lucky, Shirley. We're going to Berlin next. COP1. The first Conference of the Parties.

Don (*offering his glass for a clink*) Mr Chairman.

Estrada Don Pearlman.

They clink glasses.

ELEVEN

Don Rio had been less a conference than a product launch. Climate change is becoming an identity. Environmental NGOs start spawning everywhere, picketing UN buildings, protesting every round of talks. Friends of the Earth. Friends of the Sea. Friends of the Endangered Fucking Bumblebee. The barbarians have made it to the gates of Rome. And when Al 'Earth in the Balance' Gore reaches the White House as Clinton's VP, they make it to the goddam citadel. It's time to shift gear. In the run-up to COP1, I make sure the realities of office hit them like a May hurricane. Threaten hell and high water. And it works. They disappoint everyone with weak promises – (*Coughing.*) and vague pledges. The US remains the environmental pariah it has always been. My back begins to hurt.

Shirley I'd really like you to see a doctor . . .

Don Take your eyes off the ball for a second, they fuck you. I'm gonna attend every minute of the talks. Berlin is no exception.

Berlin. March 1995. The First Conference of the Parties – COP1.

Estrada (*addressing the Conference*) As my first duty as Chairman, it is my pleasure to introduce the President of COP1. Esteemed scientist and Germany's Environment Minister, Dr Angela Merkel.

Applause.

Germany Honecker said that 'the Wall would still be here a hundred years from now'. Just six years later, it strikes me that everyone in Berlin walks as one. So it was in Rio, and that same spirit is needed now. The Convention mentions stabilisation. Berlin asks, is that enough? The Convention set no targets and timetables. Berlin asks, how high, and how soon? The Convention allows us to adopt a protocol. Berlin asks, if not now, then when?

(*Gavelling.*) COP1 is open. The first agenda item is Rules of Procedure. I trust this is uncontroversial, so assuming consensus in the room –

She raises her gavel, but sees the Saudi Arabian flag.

The Distinguished Delegate of Saudi Arabia.

Saudi Arabia Thank you, Madam President. What are the Rules for the adoption of a protocol?

Secretariat I can explain? The Convention isn't entirely clear on the issue. It only says each country has one vote.

Saudi Arabia And what majority is required? A simple majority? Two-thirds? Three-quarters?

Secretariat That's the problem. The rules don't say.

Don Silly girl.

Don hands a note to Saudi Arabia.

Saudi Arabia We are grateful for that helpful explanation, Madam President. In light of this lack of clarity, we propose that all voting rules be bracketed.

Flags go up.

China We concur.

USA As do we.

Germany But without any voting rules, the adoption of a protocol would require full consensus, which means –

Saudi Arabia Unanimity?

Don enters the space and addresses Estrada and Germany.

Don Unanimity. One hundred and seventy countries. And if just one, even one single tiny irrelevant map stain raises its flag and objects, the Protocol is dead. That's not like winning the lottery. It's like winning ten times with the same numbers.
(*To Secretariat.*) Thanks for the heads-up, kid.

Germany Let's take a short recess so that I can confer.

Germany meets with Estrada and Secretariat.

Secretariat I'm sorry. I thought I was being helpful.

Estrada It's not your fault. I should have seen that coming.

Germany I need a briefing.

Estrada He's a lawyer.

Germany American lawyer?

Secretariat Oil lobbyist and CEO of the Climate Council.

Estrada No one knows who he works for, but you can guess.

Germany Exxon, Texaco, Shell, the oil-producing states? I've dealt with men like him my whole life. The GDR was full of them. A man like him works in the shadows. So let's drag him out into the sun.

Germany gavels the Conference to order.

Thank you, everyone. The Voting Rules will be bracketed. For now, I will continue through my agenda items, while Chairman Estrada convenes the Feedback Session for the Second Assessment Report.

She gavels and the meeting adjourns.
A side room in the Conference Centre. Estrada is about to chair the Feedback Session. A smiling, nervous scientist, Dr Ben Santer, waits to present. There is palpable excitement.

Estrada Thank you, Madam President. Delegates will remember that the first assessment helped us launch the Convention. This second one may help us adopt a protocol. If you could all please turn to Chapter Eight.

Singer, out of breath, finds Don.

Singer We have a problem.

Estrada 'Detection of Climate Change and Attribution of Causes'.

Singer There may have been a breakthrough.

Estrada I'm delighted to introduce you to Dr Ben Santer.

Singer A big one...

Santer Thanks, Raúl. As you all know, my colleagues and I working on the Lawrence Livermore National Laboratory Program for Climate Model Diagnosis and Intercomparison –

Singer You're gonna need an acronym for that one!

Santer – have been pioneering a pretty revolutionary technique called 'fingerprinting', by looking at the vertical structure of temperature –

Don Translation for the morons in the room?

Santer Oh, um. Sure. The problem with linking climate change with man-made emissions is that there's just so much damn data flying round up there, we haven't been able to find the smoking gun. The fingerprint that proves the two things are connected. Until now. Let me explain...

(*Using his whiteboard.*)

I can predict that as emissions rise, so should the temperature. And that's exactly what's been happening since the start of the industrial revolution.

Singer Correlation's not causation! Atmospheric temperature variation could as much be caused by solar flares or volcanoes.

Santer Well, exactly. So we need to find something unique. Something that only man-made emissions could produce. A fingerprint. And we found that fingerprint in the upper atmosphere, where the temperature has actually been cooling. Weird, right? Well, that's what we thought. But we were wrong. We discovered that man-made greenhouse gases like to sit, right here, in the lower atmosphere, trapping heat and causing it to warm. As more and more heat gets trapped here, in the lower atmosphere, less and less makes it back up here, to the upper atmosphere, which is why that has been cooling. The sun, a volcano, all of these other possible inputs would heat the whole atmosphere together. Nothing else could be causing this effect except for man-made greenhouse gas emissions. That's your smoking gun.

Don You know those *fuck* moments?

Santer The vertical structure of temperature. That is your fingerprint.

Don This is one of them.

Saudi Arabia We would need to study this in detail.

Santer It's all there in Chapter Eight.

Estrada What remains is to agree upon the sentence that sums up the link. 'The balance of evidence suggests a – blank – human influence on global climate.'

Don The entire chapter, our entire future, boiled down to a single sentence. A single word.

Singer So what's the blank?

Don Pretty important . . .

Singer Yeah, could be anything. 'The balance of evidence suggests a *beneficial* human influence on global climate.'

Singer We were thinking 'appreciable'.

Estrada 'The balance of evidence suggests an *appreciable* human influence on global climate.'

Saudi Arabia No, much too strong.

Santer Um . . . Except it really isn't. When you look at the science.

Saudi Arabia No, no, no!

Don I know it's weird leaving the lab – sunlight, people – but you're in the *real world* now.

Santer 'Appreciable' is accurate.

Don But it will never be agreed.

Estrada We did have a couple of other options. Observable?

Saudi Arabia Observable?

Estrada What's wrong with that?

Saudi Arabia If I look up, can I see it?

Santer Well, no –

Saudi Arabia So to whom is it observable? It isn't clear.

Santer The science. The models –

Singer Oh, the models!

Estrada Can we please *try* to find a compromise?!

Santer You can't compromise on scientific fact!

Singer There's no such thing! Only the balance of current available evidence. It used to be fact that the world was flat!

Estrada So what should the adjective be?

Don *In*appreciable.

Estrada Come now.

Don What?! One word! This is insane!

Santer Significant.

Don *In*significant.

Santer Substantive.

Don *In*substantive.

Estrada Don –

Santer Pronounced.

Don Moderate.

Santer Identifiable.

Don Inconclusive.

Santer Incontrovertible.

Don Unconfirmed.

Santer Meaningful.

Don Possible.

Santer Material.

Don Plausible.

Santer Detectable.

Don Disputable.

Santer Verifiable.

Don Minor.

Santer Measurable.

Don Minimal.

Santer Demonstrable.

Don Doubtful.

Santer Visible.

Don Arguable.

Santer Noticeable.

Don Inconceivable. Twenty-eight adjectives are proposed. Twenty-eight possible words on which the future of the human race depends. Until someone suggests:

UK Discernible.

Saudi Arabia Discernible?

Don No –

Estrada 'The balance of evidence suggests a *discernible* human influence on global climate.'

Agreement around the room.

Don A single word of weapons-grade scientific clarity. Man-made climate change has just been unbracketed.

The Conference Hall.

Germany (*gavelling*) The Distinguished Delegate of Kiribati.

Kiribati The Island States would like to propose something equally discernible.

Don Things go from bad to worse. Back in the conference hall –

Kiribati (*holding up a document*) A draft protocol.

Don One word.

Kiribati A legal agreement between all member states with binding powers of enforcement, containing targets and timetables for reducing CO_2 emissions.

Germany The Distinguished Delegate of China.

Don One single word.

China We support the Island States' protocol, as long as it contains targets and timetables for developed countries, and no commitments for developing countries.

Don One word to tie up western civilisation in a straitjacket –

China The developed world must make discernible reparations for the damage it has caused.

Don While the developing world carries on doing whatever the fuck it wants.
  (*To USA.*) Kill it. Kill it now!

USA Oh, I fucking will.

(*To Conference.*) Madam President, we object to this in the strongest possible terms. Climate change is a global problem and demands a global response.

Don One word. Restricting our growth. Crippling our economies. Impoverishing our people.

China The US has been a fully industrialised superpower for over a century, built on the limitless use of fossil fuels. Our development is only just beginning, and we will not be denied the same!

Don One word, to the biggest voluntary redistribution of wealth in history.

USA America will never agree to this. The developing world *has* to play a role.

China We oppose this!

Don A suicide note on UN-headed paper.

USA How can that be fair?

Don One word. One fucking word.

Tanzania Fair?

Germany The Distinguished Delegate of Tanzania has the floor.

Don Who the hell is that?

Tanzania Professor Mark Mwandosya. You have grown rich on the spoils of our nations. Now you drive your expensive cars to your large houses heated and cooled to an ideal temperature every day of the year. You swim in your pools and fly on your foreign holidays and eat more meat in a week than we eat in a year. Meanwhile, we cannot feed and house our people. We cannot treat them when they are sick. Educate them when they are young. Employ them when they are grown. And you talk to us about fairness? Yours are emissions of luxury. Ours are emissions of survival.

Applause from developing nations, consternation from developed nations. It descends into a shouting match.

Germany (*gavelling to order*) I'm taking a minute to confer.

Estrada This is about to fall apart.

Germany I know.

Estrada He's made it into a war between rich and poor!

Germany I know. Just let me think!

Pause.

Separate them. Shuttle Diplomacy.

Estrada Me in one room, you in the other?

Germany No. A single go-between.

Secretariat I'll set up the rooms.

Germany Make sure they have locks. And Jo? Turn up the heating. Let's sweat them out.
(*Gavelling to order.*) I'm splitting the room!

Don What? No, you can't do that!

Germany Developed nations in one room. Developing nations in the other.

Don There's no precedent for that!

Germany There's no precedent for anything. This is COP1.

Don storms through the meeting and hands a note to Saudi Arabia.

Don Say it. Now! FUCKING SAY IT!

Everyone is watching. Saudi Arabia raises their flag.

Germany The Distinguished Delegate of Saudi Arabia.

Saudi Arabia Erm . . .

(*Reading for the first time as he speaks.*) 'The President's decision to split the room does not satisfy the Convention's requirements, specifically, erm . . . Article . . .'

Don Seven! Article Seven-point . . . FUCK!

He's lost his place. Delegates turn to Don, angered. Tanzania raises their flag.

Germany The Distinguished Delegate of Tanzania.

Tanzania Tanzania would like to lodge a formal complain with the Secretariat.

Germany To what does it relate?

Tanzania To certain non-state actors on the conference floor brazenly interfering with the global multi-lateral process. Using country's delegates to propose their own amendments to UN texts without even bothering to hide their handwriting!

Kiribati AOSIS supports this complaint.

UK As do we.

Japan As do we.

Tanzania They bring the UN into disrepute. We cannot continue with these negotiations until we are certain the process is sound.

Germany I wholeheartedly agree. This meeting is adjourned.

(*Gavelling; to Don.*) And while you wait, Mr Pearlman, I highly recommend the double page feature in today's *Der Spiegel* . . .

At that moment, pieces of paper fall from the ceiling. First a couple. Then a shower. Delegates pick them up, start reading.

A little German theatrics for you.

Shirley (*entering holding one*) Donald?

Don What is it?

Shirley They're everywhere.

Hands it to Don.

It's from *Der Spiegel*.

Don What the fuck?

Shirley It's a German magazine.

Don I know what *Der Spiegel* is.

Shirley It's about *you*.

Don 'Hohepriester . . .'

Singer 'The High Priest of the Carbon Club'.

Shirley They've translated it too . . .

Don looks around and realises the article is stuck up everywhere.

Singer Have you seen? They have a photo of you with the Kuwaitis.

Don They're trying to kill me.

Singer Take it as a compliment. You've got 'em rattled.

Shirley It's an exposé. They know your history. Who you work for. They make you out to be a kind of Machiavelli. Some of the things they say . . .

Kiribati stops near Don, holding a copy of the article.

Kiribati They're right. You do have saggy jowls.

Don (*ripping it out of their hand*) Fucking give me that!

Shirley Donald!

Don Just let me do my fucking job! Get rid of them!

Don starts ripping the articles off the walls and picking them up from the floor.

Singer All of them?

Don realises that everyone is holding a copy. He rushes from person to person, grabbing it away. Shirley tries to stop him. Then she grabs him forcefully. It's surprising.

Shirley Is it true?

Don Is what true?

Shirley That you're trying to derail the negotiations.

Singer Merkel's about to start, Don! Developing countries in Room A, developed countries in Room B.

Don I don't have time for this!

Shirley Is the science clear?

Don What *science*? *Natural* science? *Political* science? *Economic* science? *Social* science? It's not the right question!

Shirley Are we on the wrong side?

Beat.

Don No, Shirley. We're not on the wrong side.

Beat.

We're not on the wrong side.

Shirley finally nods.

Shirley Then you go back in there, and you beat them.

Shirley leaves. Estrada enters.

Estrada Don –

Don I have every fucking right to be in there, Raúl, every fucking right. And you know that I know the UN Rules of

Procedure better than you and I can quote Article Seven-point-Six, Rules Six, Seven and Eight about the right of / certified NGOs –

Estrada Don, stop! You overstepped a mark in there. Delegates have lodged a formal complaint –

Don They can lodge it up their formal ass. I represent states and companies and people who deserve a fair hearing. Without me, enviros like you would sit in those rooms and trash everything good in this world –

Estrada Trash everything good in this world? If only you could hear yourself.

Don There he is! The neutral Chairman shows his true colours.

Estrada I am neutral on all matters except one. I will wrestle this process into an agreement.

Don And that is why you will fail. You honestly think you can please everyone? This isn't negotiation. It's hand-to-hand combat. Pick a side and fight for it or your enemies will destroy you.

Estrada I have no enemies.

Don Everyone needs an enemy! Even a grinning Argentinian.

Estrada What happened to the promise you made in Rio? That if the time ever came when we needed to act, you would join me.

Don We're not playing your stupid game, Raúl. This is the real world. Real consequences. I know what I'm fighting for. Do you?

Estrada Then I'm sorry. As your Chairman, I hereby ban you from the conference floor.

Don You can't do that!

Estrada Watch me.

A stand-off. Applause from the Conference Hall. Germany enters.

Germany The First Conference of the Parties has reached agreement.

Estrada Do you hear that?

Germany We will begin negotiations for a protocol.

Estrada They agreed next time to agree. *Unanimously.*

Germany This protocol will contain legally binding targets and timetables for developed countries, and no new commitments for developing countries, and must be concluded by COP3.

Estrada A protocol.

Germany (*exiting*) I hope you enjoyed your time in Berlin.

Don You sure you want to do this, Raúl? Become my enemy?

Estrada Go home, Don.

Don is left alone. The Seven Sisters enter.

Don It's time to stop messing around. It's time to burn it down. All of it. No prisoners. No mercy. Scorched fucking earth.

First Sister So what's the plan?

Don Strategy Six. Character Assassination. If you can't kill the science. Kill the scientist.

In a meeting to sign off on Ben Santer's chapter in the Second Assessment Report, I point out *discernible* word changes, *discernible* punctuation changes and *discernible* referencing changes from the version we agreed in the room. Fred makes sure this spreads like wildfire around every major newspaper on the planet. Santer is widely accused of fraud. There are calls for the IPCC to be abandoned. It's called the Serengeti Strategy. Pick off the weakest. Break up the herd. We showcase to the world a scientific community not only lacking certainty, but also fickle, vindictive and vengeful.

Santer I've received death threats.

Don We all get *death threats*. Take it as a compliment.

Santer I hear a knock at my door in the middle of the night. I go downstairs and find a dead rat on my doorstep. And a guy cursing as he screeches away in a bright yellow Hummer –

Don I don't condone / that kind of behaviour –

Santer I check under the car when I go to work. My son sleeps with a wooden sword next to his bed because he doesn't feel safe in my . . . (*Breaking down.*) *in my house*! They edit interviews with me to make it seem like a conspiracy theorist is asking whether I'm trying to 'harm world civilisation' and I say 'yes'! The Nazi Party of Germany picks that one up and re-posts it, along with my address. There are calls for my job. Dishonourable dismissal from my lab. Congressional investigations. They attempt to get me tried at The Hague for crimes against humanity! I'm a wreck. My marriage fails. I don't win the Nobel Prize. All I've ever wanted is to see this crazy, beautiful world that little bit clearer. You just want to fill it with smoke. This is how you win.

Don What's wrong with winning? All great civilisations want to win. And they fall when they begin to doubt whether it's 'right' to win. We cannot doubt America. And America cannot doubt itself. I believe America is one of the great human accomplishments. I believe in the America that adopted my family and saved their lives. I believe a strong world depends on a strong America. And I believe that the American story is not at its end. It's only just beginning.

Estrada The stage is set.

Don And I will drench it in oil. Strike the match. And set fire to the whole fucking show.

Estrada So it only takes one man to burn down the forest.

Don I don't just complain about the weather. I make my own. That's scorched earth.

Estrada (*to us*) Our friends in the Japanese delegation have generously offered to host COP3 in one of their most ancient and beautiful cities. A city famed for its peace and spirituality. Kyoto.

Don flicks his match, and the stage is consumed in fire.

End of Act One.

Act Two

TWELVE

The Kyoto International Conference Hall. December 1997. COP3.

Japan In Japan, we don't just observe four seasons like you. We observe seventy-two – *shichijuni koh* – microseasons which describe subtle changes in the birds, insects, plants and weather for every five days of the year. The most important is *sakura*, the annual cherry blossom. Nothing better symbolises the fragility of our earthly miracle.

But every year, *sakura* happens earlier. Every year, the *shichijuni koh* change. The ancient certainties of our ancestors are in flux. And who among us can say they do not notice the same? Who among us can say with certainty that we are not to blame? I therefore urge everyone here in Japan's oldest city, its ancient capital, city of ten thousand shrines, to focus on the task at hand.

Estrada (*to Conference*) Thank you, President Ohki. Distinguished delegates, ladies and gentlemen, welcome to Kyoto, to the Third Conference of the Parties. COP3. And as well as the ten thousand people present here today, I would also like to welcome the seventy million others around the world with access to the World Wide Web.

The 1990s 'dial-up' tone sounds. The back wall is suddenly filled with live images of delegates at the conference, ending on Don watching from outside the Conference Hall who we see mouth the words –

Don What the fuck?

Estrada Who, thanks to the wonders of modern technology, can watch these negotiations live over the internet. For the first time, there is no hiding from the responsibilities we bear.

(*To the image of Don.*) The world, quite literally, is watching.

Over the next ten days, it will watch these talks lead to one destination: our final plenary session. For that session, I need a draft protocol. For that draft, I need your targets and timetables. So let's not keep the world waiting!

He holds his gavel high in the air, dramatically. And then brings it crashing down on the table. COP3 has begun.

Agenda item one: the Rules of Procedure –

The Nokia ringtone sounds.

What is that? I recognise it . . .

(*He hums along.*)

Gran Vals. By Francisco Tarrega! Famous Spanish composer?

Secretariat It's a Nokia, Raúl.

Estrada A Nokia . . . ?

Secretariat A cellphone.

Estrada sees Saudi Arabia answer his phone.

Estrada Please could everyone switch off their cellphones?

Saudi Arabia hangs up and immediately raises their flag.

The Distinguished Delegate of Saudi Arabia?

Saudi Arabia What should we make, Mr Chairman, of the resolution passed by the United States Senate about our negotiations here in Kyoto?

Estrada The Distinguished Delegate of the USA.

USA That's a great question. Our senate has told us they cannot ratify any protocol unless it also includes, in some way, participation by developing countries.

Consternation from delegates around the hall.

China Which the Distinguished Delegate knows we cannot agree to!

Saudi Arabia's phone rings again.

Estrada Phones off!

Saudi Arabia hangs up and raises their flag.

Saudi Arabia And how did your Senate vote on this resolution?

USA Another great question.

Saudi Arabia Well?

USA Ninety-five to zero.

Tanzania Unanimously. They can't agree on anything apart from destroying the world.

USA We have a number of proposals we would like to discuss.

Tanzania And we look forward to hearing them.

Saudi Arabia's phone rings again.

Estrada Then let us adjourn for smaller negotiations. And we can find out what it means.

He gavels. Don steps into the space, addressing Estrada.

Don I'll tell you what it means, Raúl. Let me really lay it out for you. You can say goodbye to unanimity. Your protocol's dead before it's even been born.

Estrada You shouldn't be on the floor, Don.

Don That's right. Your rule banning me from the conference floor.

Estrada Not just you. The rule applies to all NGOs. I've had the same conversation with Greenpeace.

Don And what do you call it again, your little rule?

Estrada I don't know what you're talking about.

Don Oh, come on. You think I don't know?

Estrada I don't.

Singer (*entering*) It's the Don Pearlman Rule.

Don The Don Pearlman Rule. Truly, I'm honoured.

Singer He's written you into UN history, Don.

Don Truly, I'm honoured. But there'll be questions for you to answer after this. Freedom of speech questions.

Singer About how the UN, faced with arguments it doesn't want to hear, simply bans them.

Don I mean, what is this, Chairman Raúl?

Singer It's fucking China!

Don Not that it matters.
(*Holding up his phone.*) Me and my Nokia are with you everywhere you go.

Don gives one to Singer.

Estrada That was you.

Don The wonders of modern technology, eh, Raúl?

Estrada I was hoping for a good clean match here in Kyoto –

Don's phone rings.

Don Sorry, gotta take this.
(*Answering.*) Shirley! How's the hotel room?

Estrada and Singer exit. Shirley enters, speaking from their hotel room.

Shirley It's not a room, Don, it's a palace. You're never doing travel arrangements again.

Don This is the big one. Didn't want to risk anything on a shitty mattress.

Shirley It has a chandelier!

Don It's famous, apparently. Old.

Shirley Probably why it doesn't work.

Don What? Speak to concierge.
(*Avoiding a camera.*) Fuck off! He's got cameras following me everywhere.

Shirley That's weird. I think some guy was taking photos of me too.

Don Who? What'd he look like?

The line breaks.

Shirley? / Shirley?!

Shirley Don? Don? You're breaking up . . .

The line goes dead.

Don Fuck.

He sees USA leaving the Conference Hall.

What's the game plan?

USA sees the cameras, pulls Don close and away from them.

USA Targets are coming, Don. We have to be involved. Designing a protocol, not blocking.

Don What's the point if the Senate won't ratify?

USA Well, clearly they've fucked us, and now I'm going to have to get on my knees and beg the developing world. But if we can get some compromises from them on market mechanisms, we might stand a chance of getting it through the Senate.

Don Market mechanisms . . . You mean Emissions Trading?

USA Why ask if you already know?

Don I just love to hear you say it. We're on the same side. I'm at your service, remember? Our country's service.

Don holds out his hand. USA just smiles.

USA I'm going to be late for my meeting with the G77.

Don The Lions' Den.

As she sets off, he stops her.

It's that way. Good luck!
(*To us.*) But I get there first. She strolls into the most dangerous room at Conference where unbeknownst to her, I've been riling up the Big Cats. It doesn't start well.

THIRTEEN

The G77 plus China. Estrada observes. The USA enters, out of breath. Don is outside.

Tanzania You're late.

USA Apologies, my friends. My . . . briefing overran –

Tanzania As the new Head of the G77 plus China, Tanzania considers it a great discourtesy to keep your friends waiting. Many of us wanted to cancel the meeting altogether.

Saudi Arabia places his Nokia on a table. Outside, Don listens in.

Estrada Shall we begin?

Tanzania (*to USA*) The floor is yours.

USA We've been through many long years of negotiation together, and the first thing I want to say is the United States is here to act. But to reach the ambitious targets you rightly expect of us, we're going to need your help. So –

Tanzania Emissions Trading? We've been briefed too.

Don (*to us*) Believe me, I wasn't brief.

Saudi Arabia What is Emissions Trading?

USA It's a very simple market-based idea. Textbook cap-and-trade. We set a cap on the total amount of carbon the world can emit, then from that amount allocate per-capita tradable allowances to every developed country. Countries who reduce their emissions more quickly can sell their surplus allowance to countries who for whatever reason are going more slowly.

Don Translation: a loophole that allows rich countries to keep doing whatever the fuck they want.

China Have I understood your simple idea correctly? Instead of actually meeting your target, you want to be able to pay to keep making it bigger?

USA No, you have very much *mis*understood.

Tanzania I think I've got it. Carbon is a cake. I cut the cake into slices, and give a slice to everyone. If I eat my slice, but I still want more, then I can ask my friend to bake me another cake.

USA No, you cannot ask your friend to bake another cake. There's a finite number of / cakes –

Kiribati How about this? Carbon is a trash can. If I fill my trash can, but I still have more trash to throw away, I can pay my friend –

She gestures to China.

– to throw it into his trash can.

China You cannot throw your trash in my can. This is China's trash can.

USA Let's steer away from trash cans –

Saudi Arabia Carbon is an oil well.

USA I don't think that analogy will work –

Saudi Arabia I think I've got it. I have an oil well. You have an oil well. We all have an oil well. We all extract oil from our wells. When your well becomes empty, and mine is still full –

China You get together with your neighbours and fix the price?

USA That's very funny.

Saudi Arabia Excuse me? What did he say?

Estrada I think we may have drifted from the point . . .

Tanzania Let's be serious for a moment. If we agree to Emissions Trading –

China Which we haven't.

Tanzania *If* we agree, will that be enough to satisfy your Senate?

USA Well . . . As you know, the resolution our Senate passed severely ties our hands. They won't ratify anything we agree here unless you're involved too.

Tanzania So what are you saying?

USA I'm saying . . . We're also going to need *participation* from the developing world.

Tanzania Participation?

USA It could be Voluntary Participation, completely protecting your right to develop as we did.

Tanzania But what does participation actually mean?

China Targets and timetables.

Outrage from the G77.

Don Oh, my dear . . . You just blew it.

USA No, no, Voluntary Participation / does not mean –

Tanzania Did you sleep through the last ten years of negotiations? The Convention we signed in Rio? The Mandate in Berlin? They guarantee no targets and timetables for developing countries until the developed world cleans up its mess!

USA Without Emissions Trading and Voluntary Participation, the protocol won't be ratified. Without ratification, it won't be legally binding.

China And that is our problem because?

Kiribati It would be all of our problems!

Don (*into his phone*) Stand up and walk, stand up and walk!

Saudi Arabia (*standing*) She knows we can't agree to this, that's why she's suggesting it. I won't be party to this any longer.

China Neither will we.

They leave.

USA I'm not saying deep cuts. They could be tiny, more of a gesture, just to show the world –

Tanzania I have never been more insulted. I knew I should have cancelled this meeting.

Tanzania exits.

USA We're all in this together.

Kiribati (*exiting*) It's not about the amount!

Estrada It's the principle.

Estrada exits.

Don They maul you?

USA That was the hardest meeting of my professional life.

FOURTEEN

Don Meetings like these define the first six days of Kyoto. Nothing is achieved, not a single comma, and certainly no targets or timetables. My Nokia's become my new best friend. I can be in different places all at once. The conference hall, corridors, sushi bar and sake lounge, all without breaking a sweat.

His phone rings.

It also means Shirley can call whenever she wants.

Don answers his phone.

Shirley Donald, where are you? It's five a.m.

Don Is it . . . ? Shit. I told you this was the big one.

Shirley I know, and I'm trying to look after you! You have to sleep. You have to pace yourself.

Don I know, and I am.

Shirley Did you call Brad?

Don No, Shirl. I didn't call Brad.

Estrada (*entering*) Morning, Don.

Don There's no time.

Hangs up.

(*To us.*) Monday. Day Eight. Three days to go. And at three days to go another count begins: the number of hours awake. I say goodbye to my hotel room and its busted chandelier because today, the Ministers arrive.

UK arrives with his entourage, where he is greeted by Estrada and his cameras.

Don Britain's new Deputy Prime Minister –

Estrada (*shaking UK's hand*) Mr Prescott.

Don – flies six thousand miles from London Heathrow, releasing around three tonnes of CO_2. Did you choose beef or chicken on the plane, John?

UK Beef.

Don Another fifty kilos. Add in advisors –

UK Yep.

Don Connections?

UK Uh-huh.

Don And of course all that First Class champagne –

UK I drank tea. Two bags.

Don And he's carved himself quite the footprint.

Ministers from every country of the world arrive. Estrada greets each with a handshake as they gather for a Ministerial photograph.

Germany, two-point-seven tonnes.

Estrada (*shaking Germany's hand*) Mrs Merkel.

Don Kiribati, four thousand miles. Two tonnes. I don't know how they keep a straight face. Tanzania, six-and-a-half thousand miles, three-point-three tonnes. All of them flying, driving, eating, drinking, shitting themselves to a greener future. China, a thousand miles, nought-point-eight tonnes. Justified, they feel, by the significance of their endeavour. Saudi Arabia, Gulf Stream V, two stopovers, five-and-a-half thousand miles, one hundred and sixty-six tonnes. The Kyoto Climate Conference releases over one hundred thousand tonnes of carbon dioxide, raping the atmosphere. How did you fly, Raúl?

Estrada Economy. Like all the other tourists.

Secretariat (*to Don*) Excuse me, sir. Can you . . . ?

Don steps aside to allow Secretariat to take the Ministerial photograph, as a military helicopter sounds overhead.

Don (*shouting over the helicopter*) But when all's said and done, no one makes an entrance like the Land of the Free.

Al Gore steps forward into the ministerial line-up.

Secretariat Smile!

No one smiles as Secretariat takes the photo. USA hands Estrada a document.

USA Advance copy of his speech. I think you'll be pleasantly surprised.

Estrada Can you get me ten minutes with him?

USA I can get you five.

Japan (*to Conference*) As President of COP3, I am honoured to welcome to Kyoto the Vice President of the United States, his Excellency, Albert Gore Jr.

Gore's face fills the back wall.

Gore We came to Kyoto to find new ways to bridge our differences. In doing so, however, we must not waver in our resolve. The United States is committed to a strong, binding target that will reduce our 2010 emissions by thirty per cent –

Shocked applause from around the room.

– from what they would otherwise be.

Don Al, you sly dog. I've always said, never trust a man on the *New York Times* Best Sellers list. He goes straight into back-to-back meetings.

He approaches Gore but Estrada gets there first.

Estrada You might have fooled the crowd, Mr Vice President, but you don't fool me.

Gore Excuse me?

Estrada 'From what they would otherwise be' means you're taking 2010 as your baseline, not 1990 like everybody else!

Gore Thirty per cent is a commitment as strong or stronger than we have heard from any other country.

Estrada But it isn't a real number! What's your real number, Al?

Don (*to us*) Confused? Raúl is saying that a large amount of a large number is not necessarily larger than a small amount of a smaller number.

Still confused? Keep up. Let's break it down. When a country talks about CO_2 cuts, they mean compared to their 1990 levels. Why? 1990 was the year of the First Assessment – remember Geneva? Act One. We went there three times! No? Wow. 1990 is year zero. The baseline year that everyone agreed to.

Apart from Al. Al's using 2010 as his baseline. But why does it matter? Well, between 1990 and 2010, America's emissions will have massively increased. In fact, they'll have increased by about . . . thirty per cent. So a thirty per cent cut of their 2010 levels actually means a 1990 cut of . . .

Estrada Zero.

Don (*to us*) He got it in one.

Estrada Choppering into Kyoto with the promise of zero per cent! President Bush promised that in Rio five years ago!

Gore The imperative here is to do what we promise rather than promise what we cannot do.

Don (*to us*) This guy should run for President.

Estrada Listen to you! What happened to the man who wrote *Earth in the Balance*?! You inspired a generation, and now they're out there booing you! No wonder there's no trust anymore!

Don Remember the oath you took, Al, on the front porch of democracy: 'I do solemnly swear . . .'

Gore You don't understand the pressure, Raúl. The lobby is relentless.

Singer '. . . that I will support and defend the Constitution of the United States . . .'

Estrada You don't have to tell me! I fight it every day. We all fight it. It seems like you've just given up.

Don '. . . against all enemies, foreign and domestic . . .'

Gore I have not given up! There's just so much I have to balance here.

Singer '. . . that I will bear true faith and allegiance to the same . . .'

Estrada Only the earth, Al. Only the earth.

Don *and* **Singer** 'So help him God.'

Gore steps back out into the glare of the cameras.

Gore Let me add this. After speaking on the telephone a short time ago with President Clinton, I am instructing our delegation right now to show increased negotiating flexibility . . .

Singer Increased flexibility? What the hell does that mean?

The military helicopter roars to life offstage, ferrying Gore away.

Don It doesn't take long for Conference to realise: it means nothing. By the time Gore leaves, after fourteen hours of constant negotiation, the US is still no closer to a target. And Raúl no closer to a draft text. Two days to go, and things are going to plan. I'm winning. So, to satisfy Shirley, I take her to a temple.

FIFTEEN

The Kiyomizu Temple. Shirley enters, followed by Don on his phone.

Shirley Oh my God, Don. Look at that!

Don Uh-huh.

Shirley You can see the whole city.

Don Yeah, wow, great.

Shirley You haven't even looked.

Don There's no reception up here. I gotta call Fred.

Shirley You know who you've got to call.

Don I have enough stress already. I can't deal with Brad as well.

Shirley You should know what he's doing with his life.

Don I know what he's doing. He's working in a stupid café.

Shirley No. He's campaigning for the Democrats.

Don Are you fucking *kidding* me?

Shirley He's been too scared to tell you.

Don Does he know what I do?

Shirley I don't know, Don. Have you ever told him?

Don Wait, he's *scared* of me?

Shirley You're his father. What you think matters to him.

Don He knows I support him. As long as I can see he's working hard –

Shirley You sound just like your mother. Why does he always have to prove himself?

Don The same reason I have to prove myself! That's life! You know what, I can't do Brad right now. I have to make this call.

He exits. Shirley looks out. Observer enters behind Shirley and approaches her slowly.

Shirley So beautiful.

Observer Isn't it?

Shirley turns to see Observer.

Look at those mountains.

Shirley And all those temples.

Observer Ten thousand, I heard. Hi.

Shirley Hi . . .

Observer Kiyomizu being the most famous, of course.

Shirley You're American.

Observer You got me. You too?

Shirley Born and raised. You don't get a view like this back home.

Observer To think, all of it could have been gone because of us.

Shirley What do you mean?

Observer Kyoto was top of the list of targets for Little Boy. The first atomic bomb.

Shirley Oh my God. What made them change their mind?

Observer Henry Stimson, Secretary of State for War, honeymooned here with his wife. Persuaded Truman that erasing Kyoto might harm our global reputation.

Shirley So they erased Hiroshima instead?

Observer Imagine. All that history. All that beauty. One man.

They look out. After a moment –

Shirley Conference?

Observer Conference. I just needed a moment.

Shirley I don't blame you.

Observer What are you . . . ?

Shirley Oh, I'm just here to remind my husband to eat.

Observer What does your husband do?

Shirley I think the official title is 'NGO Observer'.

Observer (*showing her his pass*) Just like me.

Shirley Then you know.

Observer Oh, I know. You know what I also heard? This platform we're standing on. It's called the Kiyomizu *butai*, which means 'stage'. And there's a famous saying about it in Japanese: 'To jump off the stage of Kiyomizu.' It means to make a bold decision. To take the plunge.

Shirley (*looking over the edge*) Jump off there?

Observer Apparently, people used to do it all the time at great turning points in their lives. If you had a problem with your health, or needed to unburden yourself or had a big life decision to make, you would come here and jump.

Shirley That doesn't sound very healthy.

Observer No. I think the survival rate was around eighty-three per cent.

Shirley Probably why they built these barriers.

Observer Probably.

Shirley You should be a tour guide.

Pause.

So how are you enjoying the 'most important environmental conference in history'?

Observer Ah, they say that every time. Berlin. Rio. It's a long list. If I had to choose, I'd say the most important environmental conference was all the way back in 1959.

Shirley That long ago? I didn't know all this was even an issue then.

Observer Oh, yeah. It was called the Energy and Man Symposium at Columbia University, organised by the American Petroleum Institute. All the Seven Sisters were there.

Shirley The Seven Sisters?

Observer The world's seven leading oil companies. All the titans of industry. And Edward Teller –

Shirley He invented the hydrogen bomb.

Observer Exactly. He gave a speech warning everyone about what would happen if the world carried on using fossil fuels at the rate we were burning them. In one speech, he predicted global warming, the melting of the ice caps, sea-level rise and the flooding of low-lying coastal regions all over the world.

Shirley He predicted all that?

Observer All of it. In one speech. He gave the Seven Sisters quite the scare. After that, they invested billions of dollars in their own secret research. But do you want to know the really scary thing? All the discoveries our scientists are making today, all these government scientists, UN scientists, the Seven Sisters got there decades ago. 1959! Before we'd even reached the moon. By the seventies they'd correctly predicted temperature rises to the exact degree. And in 1979 they were presented with plans to prevent it all, which they then buried. They knew. And they hid it. They're still hiding it today. Isn't that kind of scary . . .

He takes out a voice recorder.

Shirley?

Shirley You're a journalist.

Observer Like I said, just an observer.

Shirley You're wrong. The science isn't clear.

Don re-enters, still buried in his phone. Then looks at the view.

Don It is beautiful. You can see the whole city from up here. And those mountains. Come on, Shirl, we got to see that waterfall. Apparently it's good for health and longevity. Might do me some good.

Shirley watches Don go. Then turns to the Observer.

Observer Ask your husband. Ask Don.

Shirley No comment.

Observer He'll tell you everything.

Shirley No comment.

Observer He's one of a kind, Shirley.

Shirley No comment.

Don (*offstage*) Shirl?

Observer He'll go down in history.

Shirley Oh, yeah? Is that why you've been following us around? Taking photographs? We're just people trying to live our lives. And you can put that on the record.

Don (*offstage*) Come on, Shirley, you gotta see this!

Shirley Coming!
(*To Observer.*) What do you want from us?

Observer Jump off the stage, Shirley. Jump off the stage.

Shirley Go fuck yourself.

He moves aside and Shirley exits. Observer shouts after her.

Observer 1959, Shirley! 1959!

SIXTEEN

Don Back at the conference centre, talks run through the night, the next day, the next night.

Observer takes a photograph of Don.

Fuck off!

Estrada I need a final figure from the EU and I need it right now.

UK Our hands are tied until we know what the US is thinking.

Don He doesn't even notice when Monday becomes Wednesday. The final day.

USA No one is getting a target out of us until we see some support for Voluntary Participation and Emissions Trading.

UK Not until we know they're not loopholes. We share the developing world's concerns.

Don For forty-eight hours he's been in constant negotiation in every room, corridor, lavatory.

Estrada Mark, I'm begging you. Can't you find some leeway here?

Tanzania The G77 is totally split. I don't know how long I can hold it together. Some want to help America –

China And some *will not*.

Don The final plenary session should be starting. And I can see it in his eyes now. Blind panic. Abject exhaustion. For the first time his moustache is uncombed. He's starting to realise: he might not have it.

Estrada Out, Don.

Don You really don't look so good, Raúl.

Estrada It's not a fashion show.

Don Don't you think you should get some sleep?

Estrada There's too much to say and too little time. Ohki?

Don is ejected. Japan locks the door and pockets the key. Don prowls outside.

USA Did he just lock the door?

Tanzania This was supposed to be a lunch meeting?

Estrada I'm afraid lunch is cancelled.

UK What the bloody hell do you mean, lunch is cancelled? Lunch cannot be cancelled!

Estrada The final plenary session should have started ten minutes ago and not a single one of you has provided me with a target or timetable.

UK So you're going to starve it out of us?

(Banging on the door.)

I'm a Minister of State! Let me out!

(Turning on Japan.)

Give me the key.

Japan Mr Prescott –

UK Give me the bloody key!

UK chases Japan around the table. Japan hides behind Estrada.

Estrada John, sit down. I didn't want to have to do this, but you have all forced my hand. In lieu of a single target from any of you, I have had no choice but to make them up myself.

(*To Secretariat.*) The documents please?

Secretariat hands out papers.

Estrada Japan, ten per cent.

Japan We cannot go above five, Mr Estrada –

Estrada The USA, fifteen per cent.

USA Fifteen per cent?!

Estrada The EU, twenty per cent.

UK Now, hang about –

Estrada And voluntary pledges from China, Tanzania, Saudi Arabia and the rest of the developing world. I'm publishing these estimates in my draft and you can explain to your governments why their public commitments are so unexpectedly high!

Saudi Arabia's phone beeps. He reads a message.

Cellphones off!

Don Drop the bomb! Drop it now!

Saudi Arabia Seeing as we all seem so open to novel approaches, I would like to present something OPEC has been working on. Compensation.

USA Say again?

Don Compensation.

Saudi Arabia If countries around the world start using less fossil fuels –

Don – which of course they must –

Saudi Arabia – we're concerned that economies like ours –

Don – which are highly dependent on such fuels –

Saudi Arabia – might suffer irreparable economic damage.

Don So . . .

Saudi Arabia We propose a compensation scheme to reimburse us for any loss of income, and to make sure our valuable fossil fuels stay underground.

Beat.

UK You're bloody joking?

Don Talk about throwing a dead cat on the table.

USA You're asking to us to make deep cuts costing untold billions of dollars, and also pay you compensation for making them?

Don What can I say? I'm a cat guy.

Saudi Arabia We think it's perfectly reasonable.

USA It's completely irrational!

UK This is exactly what happens when lunch is cancelled.

He leaves, followed by USA, China and Tanzania, leaving Estrada and Saudi Arabia alone.

Estrada Mr Al Sabban, as a fellow member of the developing world, why are you helping him destroy a protocol written for some of the most desperate people on the planet.

Saudi Arabia The Organisation of Petroleum Exporting Countries has its name for a reason. We export oil. But it is only in recent times our nations have fully controlled and benefited from it. For much of the twentieth century, Saudi Arabia's oil was owned by Californians.

Estrada Oh, come on –

Saudi Arabia Now, for the first time in our history, we can build our people the homes they need. The hospitals, roads, reservoirs, airports, schools, universities. This is our moment, Mr Chairman. And your protocol will take it away from us. As a fellow citizen of the developing world, I trust you understand this.

Estrada Of course I do, / but compensation –

Saudi Arabia Then you understand why compensation is Saudi Arabia's new bottom line.

Estrada How deep a bottom line?

Saudi Arabia As deep as the Ghawar Oil Field. We'll walk without it. And you can say goodbye to unanimity.

Saudi Arabia exits. UK re-enters with a trolley of food.

UK First rule of negotiation: find out the number for catering.

He and Estrada share the food together.

Estrada That was the last roll of the dice, John. I'm afraid it wasn't enough.

UK Keep the faith, Raúl.

Estrada Even if I get their targets. Even if, by some miracle, I get Emissions Trading and Voluntary Participation across the line. Saudi Arabia will now block without compensation. That might be checkmate.

UK My first multilateral negotiation was in 1957. I was working as a waiter in the Merchant Navy after failing me eleven-plus. Not a bad job for a thick lad from West Yorkshire, but I'll tell you this: it made me. Not only did I see there was a world outside the West Riding, but I also saw the utter contempt in which working men and women are held by their paymasters. Corrupt and exploitative, the whole bloody lot of them. So I joined the union. Got quite the reputation for being a loose cannon. Didn't help that the union brass were just as corrupt as the company men, in complete cahoots and serving their own interests. But it did mean I often drew the short straw, and was sent into impossible situations to quell the occasional uprising. My first public speech, impromptu I hasten to add, was on Goole Docks.

Estrada Goole Docks?

UK Goole Docks. To a let's say rowdy group of several thousand sailors, fuming mad and refusing to board the ships. Coups have been pulled off with less, I tell thee. I had to convince them not to strike. To go back to work. To trust in the process. Can you imagine? But I did. And they did. And every day after I faced off against friend and foe. Meetings with high and low. Turning up to unofficial two a.m. chats on pitch-black decks of boats in the middle of some faraway ocean, coming face to face with thugs armed with coshes, who twenty minutes later leave as best pals. That's negotiation. When all you've got are the words in your chest and you're an inch away from the taste of blood and the cold black sea. This is diplomacy by exhaustion. You've just got to keep walking and talking.

UK leaves.

Estrada Will you cover for me?

Secretariat Of course.

Japan Where are you going?

Estrada (*leaving*) For the most important meeting of all.

SEVENTEEN

Don (*voicemail message*) This is Donald Pearlman of the Climate Council. Please leave a message and I'll get back to you.

Voicemail beep, as Shirley enters on her cellphone.

Shirley Don, it's me. Can you call? Where are you? I'm worried about you. I think something is happening.

Don enters.

Don (*to us*) Three p.m. Three hours to go until the end of Conference, and no one has seen Chairman Estrada anywhere.

Voicemail beep.

Shirley You know I don't call unless it's an emergency. The chandelier. It's . . . flickering . . .

Don Four p.m. Two hours to go. Delegates are getting angry, searching toilet cubicles for their Chairman.

Voicemail beep.

Shirley Don, now it's moving . . . I'm scared. Can you call me?

Don Five p.m. One hour to go. Still no targets. Still no Estrada. I don't do anything but talk, smoke, talk, smoke and wait. Can't go for a shit without a lecture on chlorofluorocarbons.

Voicemail beep.

Shirley You know I don't call unless it's an emergency. Now it's swinging from side to side! Where are you, Donald?!

Don Five fifty-nine p.m. They had ten days. Ten years. Now they have ten seconds. No chairman. No draft text. No agreement. And no targets and timetables. Holy shit. It's here. Count down with me.

Shirley Is there an earthquake?

Don Five, four, three –

Shirley Nothing else is moving!

Don Two, one . . .

Shirley Donald!

Don COP3 has officially ended!

He steps forward.

That is how you win.

Shirley Oh my God – !

The chandelier crashes to the floor.

EIGHTEEN

Don It takes me an hour in standstill traffic to get back to the hotel.

Don arrives at the room. The chandelier is smashed on the floor.

Shirley It was for you.

Don Are you hurt?

Shirley No. It was for you. I knew something was going to happen here, Don. Something bad. It started in Berlin. Following us, shouting at us like we're dirt, knowing our names, you know I hate that. The way they look at us . . . Makes you paranoid. When you're walking along the street. Noticing people, cars. You start to turn off to see if they're following you. It gets into your head . . .

And I keep telling myself. You're an important man. You're doing something important. And I know politics is a blood sport, we've both been around the block, but it didn't used to be like this. When you were in the Administration we had Democrats round for dinner. We could disagree about policy but agree on the wine. There's no trust anymore. No goodwill. It's a fight to the death. And it feels like they're all enjoying it.

Don Golden age of disagreement.
  (*Making a call.*) You told me to call if I needed your help.

The First Sister enters. The others surround the stage.

First Sister Unbelievable. Just unbelievable. A reputable hotel, too. We'll be in touch with their board. Make sure a full investigation is carried out. Heads will roll, we can say that much.

(*To Don, quietly.*) Don, you might want to get back.

Don Why? The conference is over.

First Sister They're preparing the hall for the final session.

Don What final session?!

First Sister Rumour is, a draft protocol is being finalised.

Don Fuck.

Shirley Are you out of your mind?

Don makes a phone call.

First Sister He'll be safe in the Conference Centre, Mrs Pearlman.

Don Pick up the phone, Fred!

First Sister The place is crawling with secret service from just about every friendly country you can imagine. And our people talk to their people. Trust me.

Don (*hanging up*) I have to go back.

Shirley What?

Don Can you stay here with her?

First Sister You don't even need to ask, Don. It's done.

Shirley Donald, please don't –

Don I got to, Shirl. One more. Then we can go home.

Shirley But surely you can see now –

Don I have to fucking go!

Don leaves Shirley with the Sister. A pause.

Shirley Don doesn't talk about work. But I see enough to know what he's up against. These people. Talk about crazies, right? Right?

First Sister Right.

Beat.

Shirley Which one are you?

First Sister I'm sorry?

Shirley Which one are you?

First Sister What do you mean, Shirley?

Shirley Well, you're not Texaco. You're not Shell. From your accent, you must be . . . BP?

The Sister is silent.

Is it true?

First Sister Is what true, Shirley?

Shirley That you've known since 1959?

Beat.

First Sister Why don't you pack your bags? We'll get this all sorted out for you. Get you a new room. A better room.

The Sister exits.

NINETEEN

The Conference Centre.

Don Back at the Conference Centre, it's *Dawn of the fucking Dead*. There are bodies everywhere. Under tables. Under chairs. Gaunt faces. Bloodshot eyes. But the conference has ended. The cleaners have arrived. Why are people still in the building?

Singer Where the hell you been, buddy?

Don Doesn't matter. What the fuck is going on?

Singer Chaos! Delegates passing out. They've shipped thirty to the Emergency Room! Europe's at loggerheads and I just heard on good authority there 'might not be a G77 come morning'. And get this, no one has seen Chairman Estrada in over three hours. Rumour is he's jumped off the Togetsukyo Bridge! I hope you brought the popcorn, buddy, because the whole thing's falling apart! You okay?

Don rushes to Japan and Secretariat.

Don Where is he?

Secretariat Excuse me?

Don Don't fuck with me, just tell me where he is!

Japan Are you okay?

Don It's over and he knows it. This whole fucking circus should have ended seven hours ago. Seven years ago! He doesn't have targets. He doesn't have timetables. He doesn't even have a fucking text to negotiate! So where the hell is he?

Japan He's in important meetings.

Don With who? Go and get him!

Japan I can't.

Don Why not?

Japan Because he's napping!

Nearby delegates turn in shock at this, just as Estrada enters, striding confidently. Don switches to calm.

Don Good of you to make it for the end, Raúl. Think you might have a little sleep in your eye?

Estrada And now I'm refreshed, while everyone else is tired.

Don Too late. It's over.

Estrada You don't look so good, Don. Don't you think you should get some sleep?

Don You lost! Admit it.

Estrada It isn't over till the fat Chairman sings.

Don Do you take requests? 'Don't Cry for Me Argentina'?

Estrada (*gavelling an angry Conference to order*) I know the Final Session is over seven hours delayed.

Don Seven and a half!

Estrada I know we all have families waiting for us. The draft protocol is being finalised as we speak. I ask you, hold your nerve! If we can reach agreement here, tomorrow will be remembered as the Day of the . . . *atmósfera* . . .

Don Atmosphere!

Estrada Atmosphere.
(*To UK and USA.*) US. UK. Now.

The meeting breaks up.

Singer (*to Don*) Estrada's meeting Prescott and the US. Off line. No note takers.

Don I need ears in the US delegation. Find out what they're offering.

UK and Estrada meet USA in a service corridor.

Estrada Last chance. It's time to dance.

USA Depends on the tune.

UK We'll support you on Emissions Trading, if you commit to a five per cent cut.

USA Vice President Gore already promised thirty.

Estrada Real numbers!

UK A five per cent cut of your 1990 emissions. Real target.

USA We'd need the EU to match it.

UK And if we went one bigger? Could you go to six?

USA You haven't dragged me to a service corridor to ask for six.

UK Eight.

USA Not possible.

UK If we went to eight per cent, could you go to seven?

USA The EU supports this?

Estrada He wouldn't be here if it didn't.

USA Seven changes things. I'm going to have to bounce it.

Singer finds Don.

Singer Don, my source in the White House says Gore's with Clinton. And the US has just entered a secure communications room.

Don Shit. Where are they landing?

Singer Rumour is seven per cent.

Don Seven per cent?!

Singer Now we know what 'increased flexibility' means.

Estrada finds China.

Don Zhong. The US are closing in on a number.

China Does that mean they've had a breakthrough on Emissions Trading?

Don They're going to force-feed it to you whether you like it or not. And buy and sell their way out of their target.

China You cannot sell something you do not own. We will never let them turn the right to pollute into a tradable commodity.

Don So you'll walk?

China If that is what it takes.

USA back with UK and Estrada.

USA We'll go to seven per cent, but on two conditions. Emissions Trading –

UK Already agreed.

USA And Japan has to go to six.

UK Oh, come on –

USA We can't be leading the pack, but we can't be seen to be trailing either.

Estrada The Japanese have gone as far as they can.

USA (*exiting*) Then the deal's off.

UK Wait, no – !

But she's gone.

Estrada John . . . How are you going to get the Japanese to six?

Don And how are you going to get China on board with Emissions Trading? That's the real question.

UK Goole Docks, Raúl.

Don What the fuck is Goole Docks?

UK *and* **Estrada** (*exiting*) Goole Docks.

Don (*exiting*) Fred, Fred?!

Estrada meets with China, Kiribati and Tanzania. Don tries to listen in.

Estrada How's it going, Mark?

Tanzania Stalemate. China are refusing to budge.

Kiribati I won't let you do this.

China Us? Kyoto will not be China's failure, it will be theirs.

Tanzania It will be all our failures. I beg you –

China The first time western markets were imposed upon us, it was opium, not carbon, though the two seem much the same. The wars it caused destroyed our country, cost us Hong Kong and began a hundred years of national disgrace. No more. As of five months ago, Hong Kong is ours again. Our century of humiliation is over.

Kiribati We all know what it means to be colonised and oppressed. That pain will always be a part of us. But how does living in that pain help us *now*, when we can see with our own eyes the waters rising?! It will sweep away any future we hoped for when we won our independence. Instead of reliving the pain, again and again, my generation is asking how can we *use* it? What is the solution?

China exits. Kiribati follows.

How do we move forward?!

Estrada (*to Tanzania*) Keep pushing. Please.

Japan exits their meeting with UK in tears, followed by UK.

(*To UK.*) What did you do to him?

UK I told him that as conference host he was about to humiliate himself on the world stage and that in the great tradition of his Samurai ancestors he'd have no choice but to fall on his sword.

Estrada John!

UK I didn't mean literally.

Estrada He's crying!

UK But he also didn't say no.

They meet USA.

USA We good with Japan?

UK We're good.

USA You're a ball breaker, John.

Estrada But he's going to need help convincing the Japanese premier.

UK Prescott calls Blair.

USA I call Gore.

UK Blair calls Hashimoto.

USA Gore calls Clinton.

UK Clinton calls Hashimoto.

USA Where are we at with Emissions Trading?

Estrada We're working on it!

USA exits the Communications Room and comes face to face with Don.

Don Running up quite the phone bill in there.

USA Don! Can't talk, but good to see you, pal –

Don (*blocking USA's path*) How'd you get Japan to six? Who'd you sell down the river? Our steel industry? Detroit?

USA I think you may have had a little too much sake.

Don If you've gone to seven there'll be heads on pikes on Pennsylvania Avenue.

USA Always lovely to talk, Don.

Estrada (*finding Japan*) Well done, Hiroshi. Whatever you said to your Prime Minister, it worked.

Don It'll cost him dear. Hashimito's facing a confidence vote in Tokyo in the morning.

Estrada Confidence votes come and go. This legacy, your legacy, will endure. But there is one more thing you could do to ensure it.

Japan What is that . . . ?

The EU camp.

Germany Real seven, or American seven?

Don European seven? Chinese seven?

Estrada Don, this is a private meeting.

Don leaves.

Estrada Real seven.

Germany Can we even get to eight per cent?

UK Not yet. We're only at six-point-five.

Germany Greece can't go any further! Nor can Portugal.

UK Break glass in case of emergency.

Germany Pardon?

UK I'm authorised to raise the UK's individual target to twelve-point-five

Germany In which case, I'm authorised to raise Germany's target to twenty-one.

UK Twenty-one?! Fucking hell.

Germany The GDR was very inefficient in 1990 . . .

UK Which takes the EU's average to –

Estrada Eight per cent. We're there.

Germany Blair agreed to twelve-point-five?

UK He will when I tell him. He might be a smarmy git, but he gets the job done.

Germany I have to say something, John . . . I know our countries have had our differences. But seeing Britain here, working hand in hand with Germany, at the head of the EU, leading Europe as it tries to lead the world –

UK Oh, get on with it, will you?!

Germany I couldn't be prouder.

UK Thank you, Mrs Merkel. I think that's the nicest thing a politician's ever said to me.

Don (*finding UK*) What the hell is going on?

UK We have the numbers.

Don FUCK!

Singer (*entering, out of breath*) Don, it's a large British inland port on the River Humber!

Don What?!

Singer Goole Docks!

A photographer snaps a photo of them.

Don *and* **Singer** FUCK OFF!

Don My back feels warm. Each disc, up to my brain. I haven't slept in seventy-two hours.

Estrada The Final Session will begin in fifteen minutes.

Don (*to China*) They have the numbers.

China But you said –

Don It's okay. It won't survive Emissions Trading or Voluntary Participation. I'm guessing he'll start with Trading straight up, you ready for that?

Saudi Arabia arrives.

(*To Saudi Arabia.*) Where the hell have you been? I've been looking everywhere for you!

Saudi Arabia I was with the Japanese.

Don If the impossible happens, you are our final backstop. Without compensation, you object to adoption. Without unanimity, it can't go through.

Saudi Arabia Don, I need to speak with you in private.

Tannoy jingle sounds.

Don No time. Phones on!

TWENTY

Estrada Draft texts!

Estrada and Secretariat enter holding draft texts. Delegates rush to them to get a copy.

Secretariat Arabic! Mandarin! French! Russian! Spanish!

Don English, please.

Estrada hands Don a draft text. They hold each other's gaze.

Still hot. Makes my fingers fizz.

Singer Still no published targets, Don.

Don finds a TV screen, puts on a pair of interpretation earphones.

Estrada (*gavelling to order*) Welcome to the Final Session. The Conference of the Whole. We will begin with the most contentious Article, Article Three, and then move from One to Twenty-Eight sequentially.

Don (*flicking through*) Article Three, Paragraph Ten. Emissions Trading. With the paragraph, China walks. Without it, America walks. They have to walk.

And before I can compose myself –

Estrada gavels.

Estrada Article Three. Paragraph One.

Don He's off.

Tanzania raises their flag.

Estrada Tanzania has the floor.

Tanzania Where are the targets we were promised?

Estrada I'm not dealing with numbers yet. Only words.

China raises their flag.

The Distinguished Delegate of China?

Don Same point.

Estrada Same answer. No targets yet.

Kiribati raises their flag.

Will Kiribati make me repeat myself too? I'm gavelling Paragraph One.

He gavels.

Don He rattles through the paragraphs. Nine in fifteen minutes, until –

Estrada gavels.

Estrada Paragraph Ten.

Don Emissions Trading.

Estrada Emissions Trading. China has the floor.

Don Here we go.

China We object to Paragraph Ten, Mr Chairman. We propose it is removed.

Don India, Togo, Uganda, Nigeria, Vietnam, all agree with China.

Estrada Kiribati has the floor.

Kiribati We need to keep the Paragraph on Emissions Trading as written!

Don Russia, Israel, Korea, Samoa, New Zealand, all agree with Kiribati.

Estrada The USA has the floor.

USA I know we are the largest emitter! I know that! We promise to act, but I beg you: please let us keep Emissions Trading.

Don China has the floor.

China China will not allow the United States to buy its way out of its responsibilities, or dump them on the developing world. We're too strong to be brushed aside any longer!

USA You can't be a rich country and a poor country at the same time!

Don The EU has the floor.

UK We support Emissions Trading but understand the concerns. How about this for a compromise? In line two, after the words 'Emissions Trading', insert 'once', then continue as in the same sentence with the words 'the Conference of the Parties', before replacing the next two words as is 'shall define' with the words 'has defined' –

Don What? An hour has passed.

UK – and in the next line, line three, after the words 'relevant rules and guidelines', insert, 'comma, in particular' –

Don I think he's saying keep the Paragraph, but Trading can't start until Rules are agreed. Is that what he's saying?

UK Then in line four – any party, in participation of Emissions Trading – comma – upon the COP's definition of the Rules – comma – in particular for verification – comma –

Don No, I've lost it . . .

Germany Mr Chairman, we've spent twenty minutes debating a sentence without a verb?

Don It's not a sentence without a verb, it's just words.

Estrada Kiribati has the floor.

Kiribati We strongly support this amendment – comma – bringing out – comma – as it does – comma – rules / for equitable allocation of entitlements – full stop – underscore – close brackets.

Don Is anyone else hearing this?

UK Perhaps – ampersand – we could separate the paragraph – dash – from the article on commitments – comma – to create an interim arrangement – question mark?

Don (*taking off the earphones*) I think these are broken.

Germany Not without bracing the ellipsis with an apostrophe – comma – so that we can properly parenthesise the quotation mark – exclamation mark!

USA Mr Chairman – comma – we object to italicising the close brackets to colon the question mark – comma – unless the forward slash is a percentage of equitable square brackets.

China One cannot simply colon a question mark, Mr Chairman, without question marking the brackets!

USA Unless China square brackets the underscore, we will have no choice but to 'speech marks'.

Don What the fuck is going on?

Estrada My apologies, ladies and gentlemen. It's midnight. The UN interpreters' contracts have ended and they have now left the building.

Uproar around the hall.

Don You're kidding?

Estrada Find a neighbour who can help translate. We continue! The Distinguished Delegate of Kiribati.

Kiribati (*Gilbertese in bold*) **We strongly support – COMMA – bringing out – DASH – these rules – FULL STOP – UNDERSCORE – CLOSE BRACKETS.**

Germany (*German in bold*) **Perhaps we could separate the – STRICHPUNKT – from the – COMMA – paragraph to create an interim – DOPPELPUNKT – HYPHEN – EXCLAMATION MARK!**

China (*Mandarin in bold*) **Mr Chairman, China does not agree.**
    (*To USA.*) **You are having a laugh! We simply cannot – QUESTION MARK – this 'so called' – DOPPELPUNKT – without – QUESTION-MARKING this bracket** [*Kuo Hao.*]!

USA KYE WAN TSEE-OWE, Mr Chairman! Unless China KUO HAOs the DOPPELPUNKT, we will have no choice but to question mark the KUO HAO!

Tanzania (*Swahili in bold*) **Please, Mr Chairman. Instead of getting caught up in whether a QUESTION MARK is more important than a DOPPELPUNKT, or if we should KUO HAO the whole protocol, we have to remember the TUUA AIKAI!**

All TUUA AIKAI? We have to remember the TUUA AIKAI! What is TUUA AIKAI? [*Etc.*]

Saudi Arabia (*Arabic in bold*) **One moment! We must all focus on this subject matter . . .**

Pause.

DOPPELPUNKT.

Japan stands at the top table.

Estrada (*to Japan*) Mr President?

Japan My government urgently requires me in Tokyo for a confidence vote. I hereby resign as President of COP3. Sorry . . .

He exits. Shock around the room. Flags go up everywhere. Total mayhem.

Don Did he really just . . . ? How can Conference adopt a protocol without its President? Without interpreters?

Estrada (*gavelling for silence*) We continue!

Saudi Arabia (*in Arabic*) Doppelpunkt!

Germany Strichpunkt!

UK Comma semicolon punkt –

Tanzania Tuua aikai, tuua aikai!

USA Kuo hao cara-punkt!

China Comma comma –

Germany Strichpunkt question punkt –

USA Comma comma –

UK Full stop!

Kiribati Doppelpunkt –

UK Full stop!

USA KYE WAN TSEE-OWE!

Kiribati Tuua aikai! Tuua aikai! / Tuua aikai! Tuua aikai! [*Continue until end.*]

UK Full stop!

Tanzania Kuo hao! / Kuo hao! [*Continue until end.*]

Secretariat Comma comma –

Saudi Arabia Doppelpunkt! / Doppelpunkt! Doppelpunkt! [*Continue until end.*]

Germany Strichpunkt question punkt / question punkt question punkt – [*Continue until end.*]

UK Comma comma / comma comma – [*Continue until end.*]

China Ju hao –

USA Period!

China Ju hao!

USA Period!

China Ju hao!

USA Period!

China and USA continue their 'Ju hao'/'Period' duel, over:

UK Full stop. / Full stop. Full stop. Full stop. Full stop. Full stop. Full stop. Full stop.

Don No, stop it, stop it, STOP IT!

The room falls silent.

Estrada It's four a.m.! We have been debating a single paragraph for over three hours. I think we are about to blow up the whole possibility of having an agreement. I'm sorry to say we are very far away. I invite delegates to reflect on the consequences of what is about to happen. I'm suspending the meeting for five minutes for private consultations.

He gavels. The meeting adjourns.

TWENTY-ONE

Estrada meets USA and China. Don is present onstage, but not in the scene itself.

China I'm sorry, Mr Chairman. You cannot dismantle the master's house with the master's tools. We won't say it again. Delete the paragraph, or China will walk.

USA Keep the paragraph, or America will walk.

Estrada (*to USA*) Speak to Clinton. Try to find a compromise!

USA Clinton doesn't control the Senate. Without ratification it won't become law and the Protocol will be just goddam paper and ink! It may surprise you to know I actually want to do something here, not sign a cheque I know we can't cash!

China and USA turn to leave.

Estrada Can we play a game?

Don What?

Estrada Imagine this circle is our own tiny zone of agreement.

Don You're joking.

Estrada The aim of the game is for me to get us all inside this circle. To do this, I will ask you questions. If the answer is yes, we take a step towards one another. If the answer is no, we take a step apart.

Don And if they neither agree nor disagree?

Estrada (*chuckling*) Such a lawyer . . . I'll start. Do you agree that we all have responsibility for the world we live in?

The USA and China look at one another. Then break apart.

USA (*leaving*) If I leave now I might just catch my flight.

They leave Estrada alone. Apart from Don.

Don I told you they would never agree, Raúl. They're too certain.

Estrada Tribal.

Don Resolute.

Estrada Entrenched.

Don Unshakeable.

Estrada Inflexible.

Don They're human beings. They know what they're fighting for, and they will defend it at all costs.

Estrada They know what they're fighting for but not *why*. You did that.

Don I played a small part.

Estrada But you played a part. And there's no going back now.

Don And what part are you playing? What are you fighting for?

Estrada Agreement.

Don That's not a side.

Estrada Is disagreement a side?

Don That's not what I'm fighting for.

Estrada But it is the end result! And someone has to be its broker. The person who tries to take a step towards both sides, even when he hates what he sees. Who tries to understand. Find common ground. And break this habit of disagreement.

Don The person who fights for both sides is consumed by both sides.

Estrada I don't care. If one man can burn down the forest, one man can put out the fire.

Don You'll be scorched.

Estrada I know.

He gavels the Conference to order.

Thank you for your patience, ladies and gentlemen. I know it's been a long night. Please take your seats. I am keeping Emissions Trading in the protocol, with its rules to be agreed at a later date.

China (*standing, outraged*) Mr Chairman –

Estrada And Voluntary Participation will be removed from the Protocol altogether.

USA (*standing, outraged*) Mr Chairman!

Anger ignites around the hall.

Estrada It is removed! My decision is final.
(*Gavelling to order. To USA.*) I know you're not getting what you want.
(*To China.*) And I know, China, you're not getting what you want. Neither of you is getting what you want! But if you can't agree on anything, can you at least agree on that? I ask, I plead, that this commands consensus. In years to come, no one will remember what the compromise at Kyoto was. They will only remember that we did. Or that we didn't. It's up to you.

Don I look to China. Everyone looks to China.

China stands facing USA.

No flag . . . India. Saudi Arabia. Nothing. I look to America.

USA stands facing China.

No one is walking out. They're going with it. Why are they going with it?

Slowly, China and USA sit.

Estrada Then we have consensus over the Article. (*Gavelling.*) Agreed. One down. Twenty-seven to go.

A ripple of unexpected relief spreads through the hall.

Don Five a.m. Eleven hours after the conference ended, after I won, he begins Article One.

Saudi Arabia Mr Chairman!

Don Saudi Arabia tries to stall, but –

Estrada I see no consensus for that amendment, the Article remains as is.
(*Gavelling.*) Agreed!

Saudi Arabia You can't just gavel through –

Estrada I just did. Article Two.

Don Talk about high-wire fucking Chairmanship.

Estrada (*gavelling*) I see no objections, so . . . Agreed!

Shock around the hall.

We've already agreed on Article Three, thank God, so on to Article Four. The USA has the floor!

USA We object to the missing preposition in the fourth line.

Estrada The US would blow up the talks for a missing preposition?! I'm gavelling.
(*Gavelling.*) Agreed! Article Five.

Don I remember what he said to me.

Estrada Tanzania has the floor.

Tanzania Tanzania will not be taking the floor.

Estrada I think I got my flags confused. In which case, I'm gavelling.
(*Gavelling.*) Agreed!

Don I will wrestle this process into an agreement.

Estrada Article Six. I understand China's concerns but I think it's implied.
(*Gavelling.*) Agreed. Article Seven!

Saudi Arabia stands and raises its flag.

Don't even think about it, Saudi Arabia, sit down!

Don He knows whatever the outcome he'll only have enemies when he's done.

Estrada (*gavelling*) We're agreed!

Shocked laughter fills the hall.

Don I'm watching a kamikaze mission.

Estrada (*gavelling*) Agreed! Article Eight.

Don I'm watching myself.

Estrada (*gavelling*) Agreed! Article Nine.

Don And everyone is either too shocked or exhausted to stop him.

Delegates begin to join in with Estrada's 'Agreeds'.

Estrada (*gavelling*) Agreed! Article Ten.

Don Or . . .

Estrada (*gavelling*) Agreed! Article Eleven.

Don Something else . . .

Estrada (*gavelling*) Agreed! Article Twelve.

Don They fucking love it.

Estrada (*gavelling*) Agreed! Thirteen.

Don *They want to agree . . .*

Estrada (*gavelling*) Agreed! Fourteen.

A red sun rises.

Don Six fifty-four. Sunrise. Halfway through the Articles.

Estrada (*gavelling*) Agreed! Article Fifteen!

Don Seven thirty.

Estrada (*gavelling*) Agreed! Sixteen.
(*Gavelling.*) Agreed! Seventeen.
(*Gavelling.*) Agreed!

Don Nine a.m.

Estrada Article Twenty-Eight, our final Article . . .

He raises his gavel.

. . . is . . .

Don Agreed.

He gavels. Stunned delegates around the hall.

Estrada Please wait a few moments for the final targets and timetables to arrive.

TWENTY-TWO

Don He's done it. He's got a Protocol.

Shirley enters.

Shirley I know.

Don He'll move to adopt it –

Shirley I know.

Saudi Arabia enters.

Don Are you ready to block?

Shirley Don . . .

Don Do you want the exact legal wording? I have it here somewhere –

Saudi Arabia Don, my friend. Listen to me. Saudi Arabia will not block the Protocol.

Beat.

Don What?

Saudi Arabia We will not block the Protocol.

Don But . . . you have to.

Saudi Arabia No, we don't. And we won't.

Don You can't do this to me. I'm your counsel. You have to take my fucking counsel!

Shirley Don –

Don I have worked too long and too hard for this! I've staked everything –

Saudi Arabia You're a Washington attorney. We're a sovereign country. We have to consider many, many things. For you, this is your war. For us, it is only one battle.

Don sees Japan arriving back from the bullet train.

Don Japan . . . They bribed you. What did they give you?

Saudi Arabia Success in Kyoto means a great deal to our Japanese hosts. And Japan . . .

Japan Japan is a great friend of Saudi Arabia.

Saudi Arabia I'm sorry. There's always next time.

Saudi Arabia leaves Don reeling. The Sisters enter.

Shirley They're here.

First Sister Don, we just wanted to say thank you. Thank you for everything. For all your work these last ten years. It's truly been an honour.

Don I know things didn't go exactly to plan, but the Senate will never . . . and COP4 next year –

Second Sister Don't you think it might be time for you to take a step back?

Don Step back?

Second Sister Retirement. Sweet nothing!

Third Sister I'm jealous . . .

Don But I'm not finished. We're not finished.

The Sisters look at one another.

Are you . . . *firing* me?

First Sister No! Of course / we're not . . .

Fourth Sister Don, we would never . . .

Fifth Sister It's about a different direction.

Don I don't understand.

Fifth Sister Times change. And we've got to change with the times. *Beyond Petroleum.*

Sixth Sister A few of us are thinking about shifting the conversation. Some light sponsorship. Museums –

Seven Sisters Yeah!

Sixth Sister The arts . . .

Seven Sisters Yeah!

Sixth Sister Theatre!

Confused silence.

As you can see, we're still figuring it out.

Don I gave you everything.

First Sister And we are so grateful.

Don I had one more shot. One more shot to do something important.

First Sister And you have, Don. What you've done will go down in history.

Seventh Sister You've exceeded our wildest dreams. A whole ten more years of talking.

Second Sister And we're drilling eight million more barrels of oil today than the day we met.

Third Sister What a legacy.

Second Sister You've written the manual. You've invented a whole genre.

First Sister And this can has a lot more kicking in it yet. COP4.

Fifth Sister COP34.

First Sister COP234! The road is still long. And that's in no small part thanks to you.

Don No. The science. It isn't clear.

Sixth Sister You're a smart guy, Don. Don't make a fool out of yourself.

First Sister Be proud. Take Shirley on that vacation you always promised.

Second Sister Somewhere hot.

First Sister On us.

Don But it's not on you. It's all on me.

First Sister And admit it, Don. You fucking love it.

Shirley You can go now.

Second Sister You take care, Don.

First Sister Enjoy the beach.

The Sisters exit. Shirley gives Don a phone.

Call him.

Shirley exits. Don looks at the phone. Then –

Don (*to himself, practising*) Hey, son. It's morning here, so I think it's night where you are, but I thought you'd like to know. The Protocol. I think it's gonna pass. They're gonna agree. I don't know why I'm calling you . . . I don't even know if you know what I do? But whoa, this has been big. Damn near sucked the life out of me. I thought I had my hands round it, but it got away. I think . . . There comes a time in a man's life when he realises this isn't his world anymore. Look, we should talk properly, not in a shitty voicemail, but I . . . I just want to say . . . I'm proud of you, son. You're a great young man. And I can't wait to see what you do in this world. It's yours now, not mine. Goodnight, son.

Don makes a call.

Hi, son. It's Dad . . .

He hangs up.
Estrada arrives with the numbers. Secretariat hands them out.

Estrada Thank you all for waiting. You all now have the full list of targets and timetables. These numbers represent a five-point-two per cent reduction of the developed world's greenhouse gas emissions by 2010. Some may say these numbers are small. But they are numbers. And when I bring down my gavel, they will be legally binding. For the first time in human history, mankind will have agreed to act.

He raises his gavel. A deep intake of breath in the hall.

If I hear no objections, it is so decided. The Kyoto Protocol to the United Nations Framework Convention on Climate Change is recommended for adoption . . .

A silence. Time stops.

Don I look around for a flag. Any flag? But all I see is . . . *agreement.*

Estrada By *unanimity.*

Estrada brings the gavel down.

Don No one can believe it. Someone starts to clap. Then another. Then another. Everyone is clapping. Crying. Diplomats, ministers, scientists. Countries, blocs, continents. Falling to the floor in each other's arms. I've never, never seen anything like it. Agreement. Unanimous. Certain. Clear.

Estrada Like the science.

(Holds out his hand for Don to shake.)

Breath it in, Don. This is the Day of the Atmosphere.

Don shakes Estrada's hand.

Don I put my arms on my knees and my face in my hands and the world goes black.

TWENTY-THREE

A hospital ward. Shirley sits in a chair by a bed. In the bed, Don lies unconscious. The Seven Sisters appear now as ward sisters. They check Don's obs, then leave.

Shirley I'd like to tell you that Kyoto changed everything, but I think you know that's not true. I'd like to tell you that as the science became clearer, Don learned the error of his ways and became a celebrated environmentalist, but you know that isn't true either.

No, he carried on the fight. He was a lawyer. That's what he did. In 2001, he helped prevent the United States from ratifying the Kyoto Protocol, and in 2002 helped to get an IPCC Chair fired. And the COPs continue to this day. Don always said, even a child murderer deserves legal counsel. They call it zealous representation.

(*To Don.*) You sure are zealous, Don. Maybe a little over-zealous. But I don't know if you know how to do it any other way.

Pause.

Did you know that female lions live almost twice as long as males? I learned that in Nairobi. Twice as long! Not that I'm scared of being alone. I was alone for most of our marriage. Don would get up at six a.m., go to work and wouldn't come back till late at night. I spent most of my time, here or on the road, by myself.

Now, you might think that's tough, but I think it's freedom. No man to have to worry about. No man telling you what to do. Not that Don ever told me what to do. Apart from ordering my meals for me in restaurants. That used to get on my nerves.

And just like we never talked about his work, he rarely asked what I did during my hundreds of days in foreign capitals. But honestly, I did so much. Long days visiting vineyards in the French countryside. Hiking in the Swiss Alps. The Maldives. Moroccan souks. Oh, there are so many stories.

The best trip of all was to Lithuania, where Don's family were from, before they fled the pogroms. We went to visit the graves of Don's grandparents. In the end we couldn't find them, but we somehow found ourselves inside a little school. This was just after the Soviet Union had collapsed and everyone was so poor. I remember giving a little girl a banana for the first time and she ate it with the skin on. I taught the children to say hello and goodbye in English, and they taught me in Lithuanian. Sveiki and atsisveikink, I still remember. Of all the trips, that was the one I remember most.

And everywhere we went, I'd buy something. A piece of art, furniture, a textile. The house is like a living museum of the climate conference circuit.

I don't remember laughing very much. He wasn't the laughing kind. But God, he smoked. First Benson and Hedges. Then Menthol 100. Then non-menthol. Then

Carltons. Then Dunhills. Even in the car with the kids with the windows up! Can you believe that? But that's just what you did, back then. That was just what you did.

Don was weakened after Kyoto. Not as badly as Estrada, mind. 'The Hero of Kyoto' burned so many bridges he could only get into COP4 as a chauffeur! Don did have a chuckle about that. But the enviros had got their foot in the door and everything just got that bit harder.

And people looked at him different. They used to be scared of him, I always sensed that, but at some point I got the impression they were laughing at him. Then, to top it off, in 2003 Kofi Annan banned smoking in all UN buildings. That one he took really personally. But still he carried on. Attended every conference. Every summit. Every round of talks. Until one night in Bonn, when something inside him snapped.

Not snapped exactly. Disintegrated. He was in so much pain. We got back on the first flight we could. Don had to lie down all the way, said he couldn't feel his back. And for good reason. By the time they'd run tests in the hospital, they told us it had spread and that his back was literally missing. His spine had gone. And his lungs were full of smoke. Like our old car. Like the world. Six weeks later he was gone.

The Seven Sisters enter and take Don away.

But I doubt anybody wants to hear these things. They're just private memories. And Don's the only person I could share them with.

She wipes a tear away.

I wonder what that female lion does for half her life?

You probably want to know why he did it. I ask that myself sometimes. It wasn't for the money. We aren't wealthy people. I mean, we're fine, but he could have made a lot more. A lot of similar people in his position did. And it wasn't about the accolades either. He hated attention. He liked to be behind the scenes. Figuring it all out. No, it was always about something more for him.

He was suspicious of certainty. Of the instinct to conform. To follow the crowd. He believed in people. That they knew what was best. For themselves, for their families. He wanted his children to be better off than he was, like his parents before him. And I think he was suspicious of agreement too.

Remember, he came of age in a world that didn't agree. He was only an American because his parents were hunted. Hated. He believed in America. It saved them, gave him everything he had, and he was just one of its many soldiers. And he'd defend it to his death. He sat through long meetings in the Oval Office, with Ron and the other Don, in the shadow of forty thousand Soviet nukes, strategising how to keep the American people safe. I don't think he thought countries actually could agree. That people could agree. He thought we were all too different. We were designed not to be the same.

You probably want to know why he carried on even when the science became clear. To which I ask you: when did you know the science was clear? When did you decide to carry on? The truth is, that anyone who filled up at a gas station, took a plane flight, lived their lives in the 1990s and early 2000s paid Don's wages. That's just a fact.

I know, you think I'm defending the devil. But whatever you think of him, know that he was also a father. A grandfather. A husband. I don't know what it means to say that. If I'm even allowed to say that. But it feels important to say. Remember that, please.

I asked him once, early on. 'What if you're wrong? And everything they're saying is right. How will you live with yourself?' And I'll never forget, he said, quick as a flash –

Don enters.

Don I won't. I'll be dead.

Shirley And then he thought for a moment. Really thought. And he turned to me and said –

Don Shirl, this is America. We'll figure it out. We always figure it out.

They hold hands and exit.

TWENTY-FOUR

The Seven Sisters enter.

Seven Sisters
>Way up there, at the top of the Hill,
>Where fumes do fly, but time stands still,
>There exist two coloured pills.
>
>A choice to make about life itself,
>A choice between this life of wealth,
>Or a green and natural earthly health.
>
>The abundance of things, of products to hold,
>Of brand-new cars and holidays sold –
>Those guilty pleasures that never get old.
>
>Or a frugal way that lifts our souls,
>The green and fruitful valley that rolls
>Like a truck through all your worldly goals.
>
>The choice seems to lie before you,
>But you know that choice isn't true . . .
>
>Cos though our man is dead and gone,
>His oily spirit trickles on.
>The legacy of a lawyer called Don Pearlman.
>
>But he was just one of many men,
>Fossils now, they came and went –
>We could have played this with any of them.
>
>See, the Lobbyist was needed once,
>To lubricate the rusty joint
>Between business and government.

But democracy's day is nearly done.
And one day soon, the time will come
When states and companies join as one
And we'll be free to give you what you know you want.

To drive, to fly, to eat, to buy, to gorge,
To waste, to war, to order more,
And more, and more, and more, and more.

Cos there is still one truth that's true:
You require from us what you want to do.
And we shall provide, for we Sisters are you.

End.